C000139352

Tel: 01664 502860

Fax: 01664 502870

Email: JMunn96@aol.com

I+J Munn Ltd

22 Digby Drive, Beler Way

Melton Mowbray

Leicestershire LE13 0RQ

WebSite: www.tocfromjmunn.co.uk

Unconstrained organisations
Managing Sustainable Change

Unlocking the potential of people within organisations

DR TED HUTCHIN

 Thomas Telford

Published by Thomas Telford Publishing, Thomas Telford Ltd, 1 Heron Quay, London E14 4JD.
URL: http://www.thomastelford.com

Distributors for Thomas Telford books are
USA: ASCE Press, 1801 Alexander Bell Drive, Reston, VA 20191-4400, USA
Japan: Maruzen Co. Ltd, Book Department, 3–10 Nihonbashi 2-chome, Chuo-ku, Tokyo 103
Australia: DA Books and Journals, 648 Whitehorse Road, Mitcham 3132, Victoria

.

A catalogue record for this book is available from the British Library

ISBN: 0 7277 3016 9

© Ted Hutchin and Thomas Telford Limited 2001.

All rights, including translation, reserved. Except as permitted by the Copyright, Designs and Patents Act 1988, no part of this publication may be reproduced, stored in a retrieval system or transmitted in any form or by any means, electronic, mechanical, photocopying or otherwise, without the prior written permission of the Publishing Director, Thomas Telford Publishing, Thomas Telford Ltd, 1 Heron Quay, London E14 4JD.

This book is published on the understanding that the author is solely responsible for the statements made and opinions expressed in it and that its publication does not necessarily imply that such statements and/or opinions are or reflect the views or opinions of the publishers. While every effort has been made to ensure that the statements made and the opinions expressed in this publication provide a safe and accurate guide, no liability or responsibility can be accepted in this respect by the authors or publishers.

Typeset by Academic + Technical, Bristol
Printed and bound in Great Britain MPG Books, Bodmin

Acknowledgements

The author wishes to give due regard to the many people who helped in both the original research and the writing of this book. Some helped without knowing, others kept me going when I felt that I could not write another word! There are those who helped throughout the research period, from my wife Audrey and family, to colleagues in the UK such as David Marks, Oded Cohen, Jim Bowles and Mike Dinham, to those from overseas such as Kathy Austin, Dennis Marshall, Alan Leader and Dick Peschke, and of course to the people at Cranfield University with special mention for Prof. John Kay whose support, encouragement and scrutiny produced the desired result. There are those who helped to turn the academic writing into a book including most of the above and a few others notably Heening De Preez, Shaun Doherty, Neil Butterill, Jack De Gioia, Barry Urban and Tom Gronek. To these people, and all my friends and colleagues from the TOC community around the world who never allowed me to get away with unsubstantiated ideas and concepts, continually forcing me to check my assumptions again, and again, and again, I salute you. The path to unleashing imagination is not an easy one, and to all who helped me in this quest, I thank you.

Contents

CONTENTS

Introduction

This book starts with a question. Why do some people suffer from problems for which they have already developed a solution? The desire to answer this question was derived from work I was doing around 1993 in implementing solutions developed using the Theory of Constraints (TOC). This approach, rooted in the logic of cause and effect, was very attractive. It suggested that by thinking in a more focused manner, using tools developed by Dr Goldratt, the originator of the approach, breakthrough solutions could be developed and implemented. This in turn would lead to substantial improvement in the performance of the organisation, whether it be 'for profit' or 'not for profit'. I had already come across people within companies who had successfully achieved this objective, they had made a difference to the bottom line of their organisation and the crucial difference was the rigorous use of the tools contained within the TOC approach. Yet at the same time I was also very aware that worldwide the scale of implementations was very small. Although some large companies had embraced the approach, the level of activity was still miniscule compared to other tools and techniques such as activity-based costing and lean manufacturing.

It should also be noted that I have described some of the issues contained within this book already. In my first book, entitled *Enterprise-focused management*, I covered the world of project management and some of the key problems faced there. Of course the environment of the companies that took part in the research that formed the basis for that book was the same as for the companies featured in this book, though the companies were different. In this case all the companies were from mainstream manufacturing or associated consultancy practices. As a result, some parts of this book will cover similar ground.

I make no apology for that, when I see companies closed with senior managers citing the market, or the state of the pound, or some other aspect, which is supposedly completely out of their control, I am only too aware that they have simply failed. They have failed their people, they have failed their investors, they have also failed themselves. But in one sense it is not their fault, they have simply been unable to think out of the box, they have been unable to challenge the dominant paradigms of measurements and operational practices. They lack a simple thinking process that allows, demands, or challenges the way people think, and to come up with breakthrough solutions. This is what the TOC is really about, the development of people who can generate breakthrough solutions. This also implies that the set of problem-solving techniques and change management tools currently available also has to be reviewed, and challenged. Thus some of the debate that featured in my earlier work appears once more here. I apologise for the repetition but ask you, the reader, to remember that though you might think the solutions presented here to be common sense, that is precisely why I have repeated them, common sense is really not that common!

With reference to the case studies contained within this book, there was one dominant, and very interesting, aspect. At the level of the individual, I met, and came to know, people who had fully developed solutions to the problems they were experiencing at work, and in their own lives. Problems that were creating enormous pressures for something to be done, problems that seemed insurmountable, and yet they had, through the application of the TOC approach, developed a robust and implementable solution. The fascinating aspect was that having done all that work, created the way forward for both themselves and their organisation, nothing happened, they did not implement the solution.

So here was the question in more detail: if people know they have a problem they have to resolve, and they have the tools and techniques to fully develop a workable solution, one that more than addresses the problem, and they obtain the buy-in of their people, why do they still not implement that solution? The question of how to research such an issue was resolved by the acceptance of my research proposal by Cranfield University and Prof. John Kay. From the outset I wanted to use the tools of the TOC to examine the question outlined above, thus allowing the opportunity to test the power of the thinking processes of the TOC.

Given the nature of the research question it was clear that the research process would have to involve me working closely with the people I wanted to examine, which meant that the core of the research process would be a combination of case studies and action research. This in itself was relatively new for this type of research project. I also had to recognise the pressures these people were under which meant understanding the nature of the environment they were working in, the conflicting pressures to adopt any one approach over another. All of these aspects are covered within this book.

The outcome of the research process was to define a barrier to change that was to become known as *paradigm lock*. Although discussed in greater detail later, the core of this is that for a specific issue some people will find it impossible to change from one paradigm to another no matter how clear the need for such a change might be. The research also threw light on the impact the lock has on organisational development, and this too is covered later in the book.

The book is therefore a description of a journey of discovery, a journey of understanding, a journey of self-assessment and introspection. The journey is not yet complete, there is still much work to be done, much research to be undertaken. But there is hopefully a foundation here for others to build on.

CHAPTER ONE

What is an organisation trying to achieve?

Introduction

This book was driven by the need to understand the reasons that lay behind non-performance related to improvement projects. In many companies I had come across people who were struggling with the pressures of the market, the pressures of the investors, the pressures of their own management, and their own people. At all stages of the enterprise problems were popping up, and all demanding to be addressed. Over the period of time that the original research was taking place quite a number of people came through our programmes, and then went out with our support to implement carefully developed solutions. In all cases they had set themselves the target of achieving the goal or goals of the organisation, however they had been verbalised. However, it is also true that in many cases they failed to obtain the expected results, and in some cases failed to implement any change at all. These companies were all active in the manufacturing sector. They covered automotive, high-tech consumer products, manufacturing consultancy and other manufacturing areas.

Background to the research

The aim of this chapter is to introduce the environment in which the research study that forms the basis for this book took place and in which all of the companies that took part were a function. It considers briefly some of the key issues that affect manufacturing industry and some of the strategic directions companies are trying to adopt in their drive for improved performance. As noted above each of the companies that took part in the study shared at least one key objective – to improve their bottom-line performance. Whether it is measured in delivery performance, profit, return on investment, cash flow or any other appropriate measure, the aim was the same, to improve. They knew that standing still was not an option, the market and the investors had expectations that had to be met. Being manufacturing companies they knew the expectation of the market, to deliver the product on time, and in full every time. They also knew that pressures on cost would continue to grow and therefore they had to examine every aspect of their organisation to ensure that money was not being wasted, and that they could consistently meet the demands of the market in all respects.

Therefore, in each case, the people attending the various programmes taught by myself were keen to try to develop a manufacturing environment that enabled them to compete with the best in their market, to improve shareholder value, and to increase their market share. They also recognised that, although they had attempted other similar projects previously, each had fallen short of expectation, and in some cases they had not even completed the whole project. Therefore one dimension stood out, although there were many improvement projects, most if not all had failed to deliver the expected benefits. When the failure also included what I feel to be a powerful process for delivering solutions, which ought to have substantially increased their performance, then to my mind there was a real and pressing problem.

Background to the problem

Ensuring the ability to meet the demand of the market in terms of due date performance and ever shorter lead times, coupled with the never ending pressure on price, means that many companies are trying to focus on how to achieve such levels of performance without risking the company. This is usually linked to the need for very lean manufacturing environments, which has been argued by many commentators and researchers such as Pascale (1991), Schonberger (1982 and 1986), Womack, Jones and Roos (1990), and Hayes, Wheelwright and Clark (1988). In addition to being lean there is also the demand to be flexible, to be able to respond to urgent market demand. This in itself appears to create a conflict within the manufacturing function.

The emphasis today is on the ability to bring to market, on time, products that meet specification and can be made effectively within the production facility without significant problems. This emphasis is also closely allied to the goal of the company and the environment in which it exists, which in turn determines its corporate strategy. This process of improvement requires the ability to see the manufacturing function as part of the whole company and not as a single entity without reference to the rest of the organisation. It crosses all functions within the organisation, not just those directly affected by the current problem or problems.

In writing about what they called the new competitive challenge for manufacturing, Hayes and Wheelwright (1984) wrote

Studies of manufacturing firms in a variety of countries have per-suaded us that the economic problems facing US companies in the 1980s – and particularly the productivity problem – have been due less to foreign pressure and governmental pressure than to some critical weaknesses in the way that US managers have guided their companies. These weaknesses have called into question some of the basic assumptions and practices that govern the way top US manufacturing companies have reacted to their strategic challenges.

Although it is always easy to blame others, especially outside the company, the real responsibility often lies within. Hayes and Wheelwright (1984) present a powerful argument for dealing with this problem. They recognise, as does Goldratt (1990b), the problems associated with focusing on just the short-term financial measures. They argue for the development of a strategic and coherent manufacturing philosophy linked to the overall business objectives. Ishikawa (1990) considers that

Even when good improvement proposals are made, they often cannot be executed satisfactorily. Everyone rushes around shouting that they are eliminating defectives and increasing production, but in the end nothing is improved. This is because they are confusing control with improvement. If we want to make improvements we must first have total control. Only when control is sufficiently well implemented do significant improvements become possible.

Although referring to quality improvements the lesson is clear. Only when the enterprise is under control and the direction is clear can real improvements be considered. Therefore the ability to control is a key feature of any enterprise trying to achieve a goal, and improve the performance towards that achievement.

Manufacturing organisations are deemed to exist for a purpose. Their owners, in order to provide for a perceived need within the market place, create them. The owners determine the goal of the organisation whether it is making money, serving the customer or any other deemed appropriate by the owners. Buchanan and Huczynski (1985) suggest that organisations exist where individuals acting alone cannot achieve goals that are considered worthwhile pursuing. They go on to confirm that

Organisations do not have goals. Only people have goals.... Senior Managers may decide on objectives and attempt to get others to agree with them by calling them 'organisational goals'; but they are still the goals of the people who determined them in the first place.

Porter (1980) considers that the essence of formulating competitive strategy is relating a company to its environment. He then concludes that the goal of the competitive strategy for 'a business unit in an industry is to find a position in the industry where the company can best defend itself against these competitive forces or can influence them in its favor'. Porter estimates the primary forces driving industry competition to be

- suppliers
- potential entrants to the market
- buyers
- rivalry between existing firms
- substitutes

either in terms of products or services. Given these forces it is essential to develop a clear strategy to combat them. He further argues that the three primary avenues that are successful include the following: overall cost leadership, differentiation, by which he means the ability to segment the market to develop a unique position, and focus which involves target-ing either a specific market or group of people.

Goldratt and Cox (1984) argue that the overall goal of a commercial organisation is the ability to make more money now and in the future, through sales. Compared to Porter this suggests a different focus. Porter argues that the primary focus is cost control. While not suggesting that such approaches are not important, Goldratt and Cox argue that just con-centrating on cost control is not enough, the focus must be on making money not saving it, and that means sales. If the objective is about sales and therefore about the ability to meet market demand with both current and new products, then time becomes an important factor. This emphasis on reducing the manufacturing cycle time is not without reason. If, in any market, competitors are able to deliver earlier, then any company is imme-diately at a disadvantage, and that means lost sales, and that in turn can lead to closure. Therefore any technique that can reduce this time is worthy of closer examination.

Tichy (1983) suggests that 'the argument is made that an effective orga-nisation is one in which there is good strategic alignment, that is the organisational components are aligned with each other, and the political, cultural and technical systems are in good alignment with each other'. Thus developing a successful strategy involves a clear understanding of the goal of the organisation as determined by the people who own the organisation, and the ability to bring together the various elements of the organisation in a coherent structure which demands that each part of the organisation is seen as part of a chain rather than as a series of inde-pendent links. The strength of the organisation is therefore judged by the strength of the weakest link and it is here that the strategy should focus.

One such approach that has met with increasing support over the past three or four years is that of lean manufacturing. Womack, Jones and

Roos (1990) in their study of the car business highlighted the concept of lean manufacturing and defined it as follows

> *Lean production is lean because it uses less of everything compared with mass manufacturing – half the human effort, half the manufacturing space, half the investment in tools, half the engineering hours to develop a new product in half the time. Also it requires keeping far less than half the needed inventory on site, results in fewer defects and produces a greater and ever growing variety of products.*

It has to be said that many companies who embraced this approach readily in the 1980s and early 1990s are now regretting the speed with which they went lean. As the markets have recovered, the ability to use the spare capacity has gone, and with it the ability to grow the company. Lean is fine if there is no intention to grow and develop, but to my mind is fatal if growth figures somewhere in the corporate strategy.

Skinner (1974) in describing the focused factory suggested that

> *Focused manufacturing must be derived from an explicitly defined corporate strategy which has its roots in a corporate marketing plan. Therefore production people cannot make the choice of focus independently. Instead it has to be a result of a comprehensive analysis of the company's resources, strengths and weaknesses, position in the industry, assessment of competitors' moves, and forecast of future customer motives and behaviour.*

This level of focus argues implicitly for a process that delivers such focus, a process such as the Theory of Constraints.

In the same way others, notably Schonberger (1982, 1986), and Pascale (1991), have all described the need for the same degree of flexibility and ever improving performance within the manufacturing environment. Goldratt and Fox (1986) describe one method of improving such an environment with the technique known as *drum–buffer–rope*. Goldratt further examined this in 1990 with the aim of demonstrating the requirement for a clear understanding of all the factors that affect the ability of the system to meet its objectives.

Drum–Buffer–Rope (DBR) as a methodology for manufacturing

This approach has been described by many people over the last twenty years (see Stein 1996 and Goldratt 1990b). Developed initially by Dr E Goldratt as a result of his work with the software package known as OPT, this approach has been widely implemented in many major corporations around the world. All of the companies who took part in my research were implementing DBR as part of their work with myself and my team. DBR centres around the five focusing steps developed by Goldratt and Fox (1986).

These comprise the following:

Step 1 – Identify the constraint. Find the resource that is limiting the ability of the system to achieve higher performance against the goal set for it. This might be a physical constraint, or a policy constraint, or a paradigm constraint.

Step 2 – Exploit the constraint. This only applies to physical constraints and simple means; before buying more capacity make the most of the capacity you have. This might mean moving to more than one shift, allowing overtime, or changing a policy to allow more capacity.

Step 3 – Subordinate to the constraint. This means that everything in the system must support the constraint, must ensure that it functions properly. This will have an impact on the capacity of the non-constraint machines, they will have by definition more capacity that the constraint, but they must run at the same capacity as the constraint, not their own capacity. This will have an impact on many organisational efficiency measures, but measurements are not the goal.

Step 4 – Elevate the constraint. Once control has been achieved through subordination it is then essential to improve the capacity of the constraint, making sure that there is a market for the capacity, and that suppliers can meet the expected higher level of demand.

Step 5 – Prevent inertia (go back to step 1). If the constraint is no longer the constraint then it has moved and so the whole process is run one more time, and then continually, thus providing a process of on-going improvement.

Assuming a physical constraint lies within the production process, the management tool for both subordination and focus is the buffer management. The idea here is quite simple. By using time as a buffer rather than material it is possible to gain substantial focus. The setting of the buffer time is achieved by simply using the current lead-time from the constraint back to the material release point, this time being the sum of all the process time, set-up time and the time lost in breakdowns, quality problems etc. The buffer acts like a piece of rope tying the release of material to the consumption of the constraint, hence the term Drum (the constraint), Buffer and Rope or DBR.

The use of the time buffer also covers both the common cause variation and that of special cause. Goldratt makes it clear that the concept of a time buffer is designed precisely to combat the absolute predictability that some unforeseen problem will strike. The lesson is clear, with any drive to lean manufacturing, by whatever means, the dangers of such problems become extreme. The old days of excess have rightly gone away, but the safety that such excess might have been perceived to have offered needs to be met in a more powerful and less wasteful way. Skinner (1974) supports this view when he argues that 'the prevalent use of "cost" and "efficiency" as the conventional yardstick for planning, controlling and evaluating US plants played a large part in the increasing inability of many of the approximately 50 companies in my research to compete successfully'.

The organisation, if attempting to operate within the commercial environment, must demonstrate its ability to achieve the goal set for it by the owners. The responsibility for this lies within positions of management, from the board of directors down to the shop floor supervisors. Each person, irrespective of his or her position, has a responsibility to try to meet the goal of the organisation. Buchanan and Huczynski (1985) consider that

> *Organisations are concerned with performance in pursuit of their goals. The performance of an organisation as a whole determines its survival. The performance of a department determines its survival within the organisation and the amounts of resources allocated to it. The performance of individuals determines their pay and promotion prospects.*

The role of measures in the current environment

In order to determine whether the goal is being achieved or not most owners will apply a set of measures. Within the manufacturing industry these are usually net profit, return on investment and cash flow. At the end of each period the accounts are examined to determine the performance of the organisation and to see if improvement has taken place. This focus on the measures then determines the goal, as expressed by Goldratt and Cox (1984), as being to make more money now, and in the future, through sales.

However, the three measures of profit, return on investment and cash flow are usually referred to as global measures and have little or no relevance to the supervisor, operator and first line managers when it comes to making decisions. There is a need for local measures to enable people to determine the impact of their decisions on the global performance of the company. The local measures proposed by Goldratt and Fox (1986) are *throughput*, defined as sales revenue minus the cost of raw material within a time period; *investment*, defined as the cash tied up in the business; and *operating expense*, the money needed to turn investment into throughput. Perhaps the best overview of the use of measures and comparing the Theory of Constraints (TOC)-based measures to the normal cost-based measures is provided by Noreen, Smith and Mackey (1995) in their study of TOC and management accounting. More recently, Smith (2000) in her book *The measurement nightmare* and Corbett (1998) in his book *Throughput accounting* have argued eloquently for a radical shift in accounting away from the use of cost accounting for decision making to throughput accounting.

Although measures figure highly in this book as a driver for behaviour, it is not the place to delve into the delights of accounting practice, whether it be cost accounting, management accounting or throughput accounting. However, there is a clear debate between a cost focus and a throughput focus. I take the simple view that cost-based measures have lost their relevance in the environment of today. I consider that the TOC focus of throughput, investment and operating expense, and in that order for levels of importance, offers a far superior way to run a business. The basis for this opinion lies in the way in which I feel a business should be viewed. Goldratt and others within the TOC community have often made the point that organisations should be seen as a chain of inter-dependent links. This has important implications for the financial aspect. Cost-based measures assume that each link is independent and that adding weight to any link improves the whole, and cutting weight also improves the whole. But if the organisation is seen as a chain, and the notion of the weakest link is also recognised, then adding weight to already strong links does nothing for improving performance due to the impact of the weakest link. Equally cutting weight has little impact on the strong links and devastating impact if the weakest is cut. As those proposing cost-based measures lack the five focusing steps of TOC they have no idea where to cut, therefore are almost certain to attack the wrong point. There are other implications and observations that could be made, suffice to add that a focus of throughput, linked to the notion of the weakest link, or constraint, offers a far better way forward, and a safer one. Thus if we take the notion of dependent links, as in a chain, and the concept of the weakest link and the five steps of focusing, then the model that allows for the best view of any organisation is that of the revenue chain.

The notion of the revenue chain

To my mind, the revenue chain is a key aspect of the holistic approach of the TOC. The chain stretches from the supply base through the company to the market. Money flows from the market back through the chain, just as material, from raw to finished goods, flows in the opposite direction. This is shown in Fig. 1.1.

The chain will contain all the key functions within the enterprise. Starting with the supply, the flow of material and/or information enters the company.

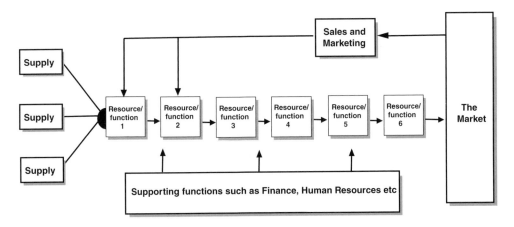

Fig. 1.1. A simple revenue chain

It might be straight on to the shop floor, it might be into a raw material warehouse, it might even be to product development: from the entry point the product flows through the organisation and on out to the market. When working in companies this process of mapping the flow of both material and money is vital if the real impact of the problems facing the company is to be properly addressed. Once the process has been mapped the next stage is to determine the various problems that exist at each point along the way. By asking people just what it is they have to struggle with each and every day a picture soon appears. Equally it is necessary to determine the financial impact by asking for quantification in monetary terms of these problems and then to add them up. In one company this activity led to the recognition that each year over £6m was lost in real money as a result of failing to address the problem set that existed. Of course there had been many attempts to deal with these problems, but always in isolation. For almost every problem it was possible to identify a project that set out to remove the problem, to overcome it and prevent it from having any impact. However, it was also clear that most of these so-called improvement projects had failed. The reason for the failure was the concurrent failure to properly analyse the problems in the first place. They were almost always symptoms of deeper problems within the company, but no attempt had been made to determine the causes of these many, and malicious, effects. Hence the importance of coupling the five steps of focusing described earlier to the power of the thinking processes of the TOC.

The role of change

If this were all that concerned managers, although appearing tough, it would not be impossible; however, there is also the fact that change is taking place. Likert (1967) argued

> *Every organisation is in a continuous state of change. Sometimes the changes are great, sometimes small, but change is always taking place. The conditions requiring these changes arise from both within and without. As a consequence there is a never-ending need for decisions, which guide adjustments to change. The adequacy of these decisions for meeting an organisation's current and developing internal and external situations determines the well-being, power and future of that organisation.*

If the statement expressed by Skinner (1974) earlier is accepted, that many of the rules and measures etc. used in most organisations are erroneous, then, when linked to the notion that measurements should motivate the people within the various parts of the organisation to do what is best for the organisation as a whole, some measurements do not achieve that purpose at all. They do not induce people to do what is good for the organisation. At the same time, if training conditions people, and there is a lot of training taking place, based on the erroneous factors already described then it is very likely that many people are conditioned to follow rules, even erroneous ones. Of course, the intuition most people have is very strong so there is the real possibility that many people are, at least subconsciously, disagreeing with their own actions. If people are rewarded according to their performance versus the measurements, and these same measurements are also erroneous, then people are forced to behave in line with some erroneous measurements and often find themselves valued somewhat arbitrarily.

This leads to two conclusions. The first is that if people find themselves at odds with their intuition, yet are forced to behave that way, then they find they are in conflict with common sense. Also if they feel valued in that way then some will feel that they are undervalued while others are overvalued. Given that satisfaction is important to people then frustration is a normal outcome. As this then requires an outlet people start to finger-point and the blame culture becomes apparent, or some people just give up and become apathetic. If there is a real sense of injustice then the like-lihood is that there will be considerable activity behind the scenes and political manoeuvring. This in turn leads to a sense of protecting one's back and the whole scenario leads to walls of distrust between levels and functions.

The outcome of this rigid application of measures and rules, coupled with training and education based on erroneous assumptions, is a company that is facing real difficulties and certainly has no real chance of improving performance in the long term. Tichy (1983) has proposed one response to this problem. He considers that

> The response to managing in turbulent times requires organisations to return to basic questions about their nature and purposes. The fundamental character of their technical system will need re-examination resulting in new missions and strategies, major re-structuring and revamping of the financial, marketing, production, and human resource systems. Organisations' political systems as reflected in who gets ahead, how they get rewarded, and who has power to make decisions would also need overhaul. Organisations' cultures are perhaps the most complex and subtle yet most pervasive on their effectiveness. Thus major change will require addressing issues of values and beliefs of organisation members.

Tichy is referring to the need in times of economic and political turbulence for the ability continually to examine the direction and nature of the organisation. This must include a review of the basic assumptions that led to the formation of the organisation in the first place. In turn, this should cover the cultural, political and technological dimensions of the company and include all the people within it. The review ought to go right to the heart of the organisation and challenge these basic assumptions. It also requires the examination of the many causalities that exist, teasing out the real and the erroneous, and starting the organisation once more on a process of on-going improvement.

This final statement, concerning on-going improvement, is found throughout the writings of people such as Goldratt (1990a), Deming (1986), Imai (1986) and Feigenbaum (1991). They each recognise the importance of ensuring that performance is continually reviewed and upgraded. For them any organisation that did not improve was already slipping behind the competition, hence the need to analyse performance, seek out the areas of non-performance and deal with them properly. This is the starting point for such approaches as the 14 points of Deming, the statistical approaches of Feigenbaum, the Kaizen described by Imai and the TOC of Goldratt.

Putting the debate into a TOC context

The discussion so far has shown that there are two key elements in determining the operational success of an organisation. Assuming the goal has been defined, and this is not always the case, and the measures appropriate to the goal also defined, then progress towards the goal can be measured. Fine so far, however, from the debate, two clear, distinct and potentially conflicting choices appear. The first is to focus on what might be described as the *corporate focus* where cost and the issues of cost allocation and profit allocation are paramount. What within the TOC community is called the *cost world*. The other side is where the focus is very much on satisfying the needs of the market – the *market focus* – the area where sales are seen as paramount. Within the TOC community this is known as the *throughput world*. In the current environment these are seen as choices. At one moment in time one of the two will be chosen as the primary focus, but events could easily switch that focus to the other. This is an excellent example of a choice cloud.

Clouds and the creation of understanding

The term *clouds*, or to give it the full term as described by Dr Goldratt, *evaporating clouds*, is drawn from the book by Richard Bach (1977) entitled *Illusions*. In the book one of the characters attempts to eradicate clouds through the use of thinking, in fact the term in the book is *vaporising clouds* which to my mind is stronger and more positive than evaporating clouds. Vaporising involves a clear physical effort to achieve the task, while evaporating will happen over time anyway. So I prefer vaporising clouds. The structure of the basic cloud is shown in Fig. 1.2.

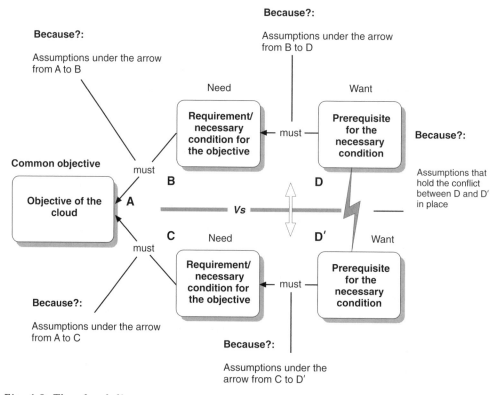

Fig. 1.2. The cloud diagram

The main boxes, entitled **A**, **B**, **C**, **D** and **D′**, make up the main structure of the cloud. The logic of the cloud is that of necessity. Thus **A** is the objective of the cloud and both **B** and **C** are the necessary conditions that are required for the objective to be realised. These are defined as necessary conditions but are not always sufficient in themselves for the existence of the objective. In the same manner **D** is the necessary condition for **B** and likewise **D′** for **C**. The conflict exists between **D** and **D′**. Once the cloud has been verbalised in this way the next stage is to ensure that the logic holds true by reading the cloud and amending the verbalisation where necessary. The cloud is read from the tip of the arrow to the tail. For example, 'in order to have (A) I must have (B); in order to have (A) I must have (C)'. The rest of the cloud is read in the same manner.

Once the verbalisation of the cloud is clear the next step is to surface the assumptions that lie beneath every arrow. This is done by adding the word 'because' after the phrases above. For example, 'In order to have (C) I must have (D′) because...'. The assumptions that are surfaced are then placed in the appropriate box. The next step is to examine the assumptions to see which of them are erroneous and which are not. If an assumption is found to be erroneous then it may be possible to break the seemingly unbreakable conflict that exists. In this way the cloud is broken and the objective can be reached. This would then involve other tools of the TOC/TP (Theory of Constraints/Thinking Processes). I have said that the present situation involves a choice cloud. Using the basic structure described above results in Fig. 1.3.

If we read the cloud properly then this is what it says

> In order to achieve the goal of the organisation we must maintain our corporate focus. Also in order to achieve the goal of the organisation we must maintain our market focus. In order to maintain our corporate focus we must use the cost-based measures that are common throughout our industry. However in order to maintain our market focus we must use sales-based measures.

Now constructing the cloud is not enough, we must also check to see just how powerful the conflict is between what is written in the **D** box and what is written in the **D′** box. This can be done by checking the impact of **D** on **C** and the impact of **D′** on **B**. If we start with the **D** on **C** connection, what is clear is that many companies, in using cost-based measures actually destroy their capability to grow sales. Equally, if we focus on the sales-based measures, it is also clear that those doing so fall foul of the corporate measurement system. Goldratt and Cox demonstrate this very conflict in the first chapter of the book *The goal* in the example of Mr. Peach focusing on one particular customer and not even thinking about efficiencies and other cost-based measures. Only later, when he is explaining the

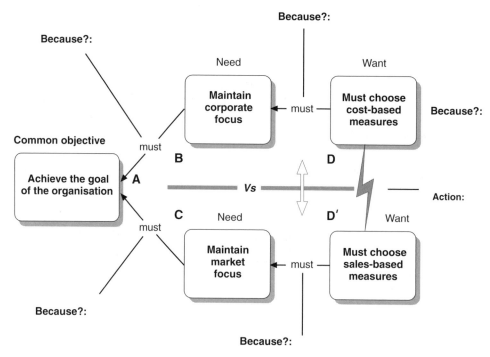

Fig. 1.3. The choice cloud

difficulties the plant is in does he revert to the use of cost-based measures with which to challenge Alex Rogo. This cloud is therefore, to my mind, one of the ultimate choice clouds. If I choose one side of the cloud the other is immediately excluded and vice versa.

The choice cloud is, however, the first in a hierarchy of clouds. The choice cloud sits as the driver for the hierarchy, it then drives a decision cloud, the conflict between one side and the other. This is a clear decision and has to be a conflict, it is impossible to choose both sides of the cloud at the same time. For this choice cloud the decision cloud might look like that shown in Fig. 1.4.

Having made a decision there is the third in this hierarchy of clouds – the conflict of subordination cloud. Decisions are supposed to be followed, but what happens when following the decisions makes no sense in the mind of the person responsible for implementing the decision? Here is a real conflict once more – that of subordination. Often people in the various programmes I run observe that they have to implement the cost-based, efficiency-based measures, however, once clients complain they have to switch to the other side of the cloud and work according to sales-based measures. This switching from side to side only confirms the inadequacy of senior management to really focus on what is important.

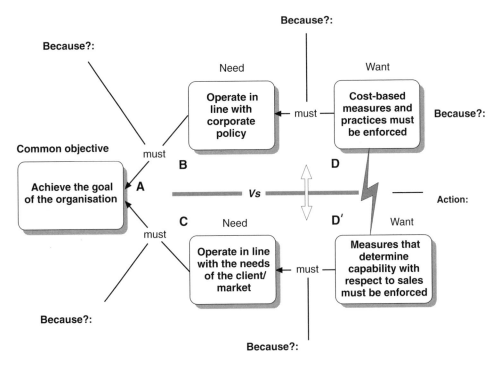

Fig. 1.4. The decision cloud

The question that needs to be answered

Given all the available approaches to improvement that exist, including some of those described earlier, one would expect to find many organisations experiencing rapid and sustained growth. The reality is that many organisations find that the expected improvements do not appear. This suggests that there is a further obstacle to improvement not defined in the usual methods adopted. If it is accepted that most, if not all, improvements involve change, often significant change, then the combination of a need to improve with the requirement to change, suggests that the obstacle concerned lies with the people involved. If this is the case then it can be argued that, given the need for change, the behaviour appears dysfunctional. The observable effect, which prompts this problem, is that of a dysfunctional constraint preventing an individual from implementing a solution. The question is what kind of dysfunctional constraint is this. Can it be determined, described, and if so can it be done in such a way as to both illuminate and suggest a way to alleviate the impact of this constraint?

I have tried to describe this in the form of a third cloud (Fig. 1.5), it is actually the first cloud but with one key question about the relationship between **D** and **D'**, just what is it that keeps these two in conflict? Is it

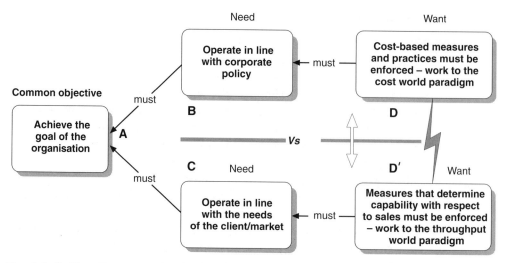

Fig. 1.5. Setting the research question

possible to have sales-based measures that do not compromise the corporate focus in any way? If that were the case then it would be possible to have the right level of corporate focus, the right level of market focus and achieve the goal of the business.

If we can determine why these two are in conflict, why is it so difficult to move from one paradigm, that of the cost world, to a different paradigm, that of the throughput world? Just what is the precise reason for people holding to measures that plainly do not work, while at the same time eagerly seeking the ability to move to a better set of measures which not only meet the requirements of the business but that of the market as well?

Why bother?

The research, and the writing of this book, was justified by the importance of understanding the process by which people tasked with managing a change programme within their organisation actually do so. This is linked to determining the causes for the creation and maintenance of personal obstacles in the change process. If there are obstacles, which prevent the successful outcome, then they need to be identified and solutions developed. The whole area of change has attracted a great deal of research and analysis in many countries. Although this has been introduced already within this chapter it will be discussed in more detail in chapter 2. Finally, it is intended that those tasked with examining the area of change and change management will be able to build on the results of the research outlined in this book in their own field.

Some key assumptions

For the purposes of the research a number of basic assumptions were made. These refer primarily to the programmes being attended but in turn also apply to this research. First, that all of those attending the programmes were seeking to improve the performance of their organisations. Second, that the measures used to determine the improvement were, at the commencement of the programmes, rooted in the cost-based approaches, any change to throughput-based measures not yet having been taken. Third, that the people attending the programmes included those who had the position and authority to implement the required changes at the appropriate time. Fourth, that those attending the programmes had sound intuition about their organisation, the products they made, and the processes that were used to do so and the markets they were aiming at. Indeed the assumption is that they had sound intuition about all aspects of their company and the environment in which it operated. Fifth, that they cared about their company and the people who worked there and that they were not seeking to use the skills and techniques taught as part of the programmes to simply cut cost by laying people off. The five basic assumptions exist prior to any programme and were deemed to be true of all those attending, unless proven otherwise.

Each person attending, and in particular the senior managers and directors, came to the programme seeking improvement in their organisation and, in some cases, their own performance. Although they began with a desire to deal with at least one specific function or area of their business, they each recognised that the core issues they were dealing with centred on their ability to solve problems. Although each problem was related to at least one function within the business, and others crossed functions, the key issues that the programmes focused on were those of problem solving, decision making and the implementation of solutions.

One final thought for this chapter. To my mind there is only one key constraint in any organisation. If the intention is to substantially increase throughput I have discovered only one genuine constraint. It is not the market, it is not capacity, it is not the size of the warehouse, it is not a lack of people, and it is not a lack of money. In fact it is not the lack of anything except one dimension that only human beings can bring. Sure the rest all seem to be potential constraints. To my mind these are only obstacles on the path to the goal. They can all be overcome if, and it is a big if, we unleash the intuition of our people. The only constraint to my mind is a lack of imagination. This book, the research that lies behind it, the TOC/TP tools are all about allowing people, from board room to shopfloor to think. To release the energy of the mind.

CHAPTER TWO

Assessing the current approaches to resolving problems

This whole area also figured strongly in my earlier work, that of *Enterprise-focused management* and much of what is written here also appeared in that book.

Improvement projects are designed to deal with a problem. The starting point is the recognition that a problem exists. This leads to a careful analysis of the problem and from that to develop a solution. Once the solution has been determined it is important to implement it properly. This usually involves change, from a small minor adjustment to considerable upheaval throughout the whole organisation. To be successful this change must be properly managed. This cycle of problem–solution–implementation is also linked to the ability of the organisation to learn, from both failure and success.

This then sets the tone and content of this chapter. If the research sets out to examine why improvement projects fail, then it is important to examine the process by which the individual determines his or her plan of action. Hence an overview of the common approaches to problem solving and solution development acts as a check to ensure that those taking part in the research followed commonly accepted practice. Once this has been covered it is important to check the literature concerning the management of change to see what is said about the potential barriers to successful change. This in turn leads to the ability of the organisation to learn. What are the factors that lead to successful change and which prevent it? Dealing with problems and managing change have been part of organisations since they began. In many cases the problems are not new and the need for change, and indeed the change itself, is not new. Therefore it can be argued that organisations, to be really effective, must learn from these problems such that they do not occur again.

The approach adopted in this research for problem solving, managing change and their wider dissemination was the TOC/TP, a description of which appears later in the chapter.

A re-examination of problem-solving tools

There are a great number of problem-solving tools available to managers.

Some are clearly in the realm of mind-mapping and brain-dumping. Others are more focused and offer a methodology that is expected to produce solutions to what might at first appear to be fuzzy problems. Before considering the TOC approach it is useful to have some idea of the range of techniques available. What follows is a brief overview of other techniques and tools currently available, but first just what is a problem?

Newman (1995) defines problems in four ways.

> *A performance deviation is where something odd or unexpected has occurred. A matter of difference is the gap between where we are, and where we want to go.*

He then adds two further aspects

> *An open problem is one without a correct solution and a closed problem is one, which can be precisely defined, and has clear parameters and a correct solution.*

In the sense of this research, the types of problems being discussed are often seen to be open. There is no clear solution. Indeed where the deeper questions raised by the research are concerned, the individual is almost always convinced that there is no solution. They are also convinced that the gap is too large, that there is no process that can bridge the gap. Newman recognises the impact that mindset can have on this element of problem solving. He also recognises the importance of learning through problem solving.

For Newman, the first stage is to define the problem. He then discusses a number of techniques to do just that. Newman describes analytical tools such as fishbone diagrams, multiple cause diagrams and force field analysis as viable tools for achieving the level of understanding required. Once the data has been analysed, Newman suggests using such techniques as brainstorming for the generation of solutions. When a number of potential solutions have been identified it is then necessary to choose one. Once this task has been accomplished it is then necessary to implement the solution.

VanGundy (1988) has defined a problem as '. . . any situation in which a gap is perceived to exist between what is and what should be. If an actual and a desired state are viewed as identical, then no problem exists.' VanGundy summarises the preconditions he feels are necessary in order to begin the problem-solving process as being

> *(1) the existence of a gap between what is and what should be*
> *(2) an awareness that a gap exists*
> *(3) the motivation to decrease the gap*

(4) an ability to measure the size of the gap
(5) the abilities and resources required to close the gap.

VanGundy describes what is almost the definitive sequence of events in problem solving. Starting with problem analysis and redefinition, through idea generation to idea evaluation and selection and ending in implementation, this sequence is deemed to be the norm. He and Newman describe a whole range of potential methods that can be used, but they are all stand-alone. This suggests that a more systematic approach would be of greater value. One such approach is that proposed and outlined by Checkland (1981) and Checkland and Scholes (1990) called *Soft systems methodology*, which will be discussed later.

Newell and Simon (1972) suggested that human cognition be based on the ability of the individual to process information. This includes the ability to store and retrieve information from long-term memory, and at the same time have the capacity to handle information in short-term memory. This led to the recognition of two key phases in problem solving, identifying the problem space, and being able to use some form of means/ends analysis for solutions. The first element is part of the intuition and knowledge of the individual, being able to recognise problems, or the patterns that determine problems, based on the previous experience of Newell. The second element is about the ability to determine, or select, actions, that take the individual closer to their goal. These actions are then implemented.

Of course, for many situations, more than one type of action is possible and it is not always feasible to either remember each one, or to determine the impact it might have. There are also occasions when the correct path is to take actions that appear to move away from the goal, but which are in fact necessary in order to achieve the goal. These actions can often be in conflict with accepted practice.

Newell and Simon (1972) indicated several ways in which the second element could be successfully implemented. These include: specifying and attaining sub-goals, working backwards from the goal to the solution, using old analogous solutions on the current problems and using diagrams of various sorts to delineate the problem space. The role of intuition is recognised as vital if the initial analysis is to have any merit. The ability to properly define the problem space, and thus the core problem, is the first step in determining the solution.

The approach described by Bransford and Stein (1984) known as the ideal problem solver recognises the importance of finding assumptions that might be limiting the problem resolution. They consider a number of mechanisms for the surfacing of assumptions such as making prediction, seeking criticism and others.

The application of the soft systems methodology in problem solving

Checkland (1981) sets his problem-solving methodology into a scientific context. Drawing on the research developed in the area of general systems theory, Checkland considers the importance of placing problem solving firmly in the scientific domain. For Checkland, the importance of applying the scientific approach is in the determination of explanations which, for him, 'requires the elucidation of chains of causes and effects, and testable prediction'. For Checkland, logical analysis is a vital part of understanding what is happening within the system. He does sound one note of caution, however. He writes that 'scientifically acquired and tested knowledge is not knowledge of reality, it is knowledge of the best description of reality that we have at that moment in time'. Checkland argues strongly that 'science is an enquiring or learning system'. He goes on to state

> Science is a way of acquiring publicly testable knowledge of the world, it is characterised by the application of rational thinking to experience, such as is derived from observation and from deliberately designed experiments.

This application of the scientific method is a key feature of the approach adopted by Checkland. In terms of hypotheses, he argues that 'a hypothesis refuted is a more valuable experimental result than one in which the hypothesis survives the test'. Given this background in the scientific method Checkland developed his approach to problem solving as comprising the following steps.

(1) the problem situation: unstructured
(2) the problem situation: expressed
(3) root definitions of the relevant systems
(4) conceptual models comprising both a formal system concept and other systems thinking
(5) a comparison between the conceptual model and the problem situation
(6) the development of feasible and/or desirable changes
(7) the action(s) to improve the problem situation.

What is clear from the work of Checkland (1981) and Checkland and Scholes (1990) and Katz and Kahn (1978) is that the systems approach differs greatly from that of Newman (1995) and VanGundy (1988). The systems approach takes note of the causality that exists within organisations. This is very much in line with the TOC/TP approach that demands the viewing of the organisation as a series of links in a chain whereas that of Newman and VanGundy makes no such assumptions. The traditional approach considers each link in the organisation to be separate and that the improvement of any one will lead to an overall improvement. The systems approach, with the focus on the links being part of a chain, notes the importance of the interdependence of the links and argues that this must be taken into consideration when trying to deal with problems.

Goldratt (1997) argues that if the organisation must be viewed as a series of links in a chain, then the efforts in terms of solving problems must be focused on the weakest link in the chain. Equally, any actions that are taken as a result of the problem will inevitably have impact elsewhere, due to the linkages. Therefore the importance of managing the change process assumes a greater degree of significance. If the impact was in only one area with little or no impact in any other area then the process of change would be primarily in that one area. If there are linkages, the change process will impact a far wider environment than before and create new problems, in particular the need to resolve potential conflict.

Recognition of this impact means that anyone attempting to use the TOC/TP approach to problem solving must be aware of the systemic nature of the process. This requires a careful understanding of many of the key issues raised by managing a change process.

The Theory of Constraints approach to problem solving

This research uses the problem-solving approach developed by Dr Goldratt. The approach centres on the need to answer three questions, What to change? What to change to? and How to effect the change? This is very much in line with the approaches already described. As part of the first stage the individual starts with the undesirable effects within his or her area of control and through the use of effect–cause–effect logic builds a picture of current reality that determines the core problem under review. Once the core problem has been determined it is necessary to build a picture of the solution through the use of the same logic this time building the future reality analysis. The final question involves the use of logic to determine the implementation path including key milestones. The approach depends heavily on the intuition of the people building the logic and their desire to deal with the problems they are experiencing.

Stein (1996), Levinson (1998), Dettmer (1997) and Scheinkopf (1999) have all described the step-by-step approach contained with the TOC/TP in some detail. This research is not concerned with the details of the TOC/TP approach to problem solving and change management although it will use one of the thinking process tools, the cloud, as part of the analysis. This technique was first introduced in chapter 1.

Managing change

Brooks (1980) described the elements of organisational change as shown in Fig. 2.1.

From this Brooks derives five major areas which management must take into account if it is to aid rather than hinder organisational change. Brooks considers that 'the model provides a conceptual framework which focuses on the key variables influencing the success or otherwise of management change initiatives'. These five are the aims and objectives of management, the technology being applied, the people involved, the current structure, and the range of control in the environment.

Of course when considering the forces that act on organisations, the structure of that organisation has important connotations for the way in which it responds. It is implied that if the organisation and the environment in which it exists are about to change then it is equally likely to require a change within itself in terms of structure and culture if it is to remain responsive and adaptive. There have been many studies which show that there are many effective organisations operating in stable environments or with stable technologies that are characterised by rigid structures with power concentrated at the top and clearly defined roles at lower levels. It is equally true to say that where the environment is rapidly changing then the effective organisation is characterised by less reliance on formality and greater reliance on interdependence of unit operation. This is coupled with greater emphasis on joint planning and problem solving with greater responsibility and authority placed at

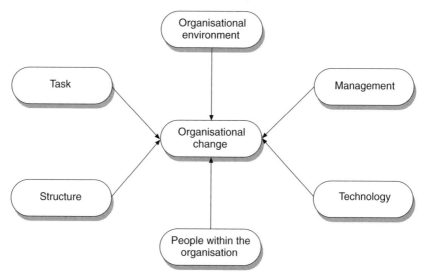

Fig. 2.1. Brooks organisational change model

lower levels. (Burns and Stalker 1966; Emery and Trist 1965; Lawrence and Lorsch 1967; Pettigrew and Whipp 1991).

Thus if an organisation is in the process of change, fixed rules and procedures will rapidly become outdated and severely hinder the process. As change often involves the unexpected, with unforeseen influences, a joint participative approach is to be preferred, as is the case with the TOC/TP methodology. Of course some organisations still feel that change will not affect them. This opinion is dismissed by Hersey and Blanchard (1972) who take the view that such is the nature of a dynamic society that the question of change has shifted from whether it will happen to one of when. They state

> ... how do managers cope with the inevitable barrage of changes, which confront them daily in attempting to keep their organisations viable and current. While change is a fact of life, effective managers... can no longer be content to let change occur as it will, they must be able to develop strategies to plan, direct and control change.

The risks associated with change

The fact that change has become commonplace involves the organisation in risk-taking. Moore and Gergen (1985) place risk-taking as

> ... a crucial element in change, transition and entrepreneurship. In turn, fear of risks is a key factor in resistance to change both for managers who need to decide whether or not to initiate change and for employees required to adapt for change.

Thus risk has two primary elements, the risk to the organisation and the risk to the individual. Both of these are recognised by Moore and Gergen who then outline four key structural/cultural factors that influence risk-taking. These can be summarised as follows

- Organisational expectations where the managers need to clarify what changes need to occur, why they are necessary and what is expected as a result of those changes.
- Reward systems, whether formal or informal.
- Support systems, which apply to the entire workforce.
- Available resources to allow the risk taker to discover a working system.

In order to achieve change Moore and Gergen consider that organisations need moderately high-risk takers and it is this risk that requires careful consideration. They conclude by saying

> *Asking people to change is asking them to innovate: to try new tasks,*
> *skills and work methods at all levels to make the change work well for*
> *themselves and the organisation.*

The challenges of change

Risk is not the only challenge facing managers when change is required. Leonard-Barton and Kraus (1985) identify a number of key challenges which include the dual role within the company of those involved with the task of change, the variety of internal markets to be served, legitimate resistance to change, the right degree of promotion, the choice of the implementation site, where appropriate, and the need for one person to take responsibility. In consideration of the dual role they note that

> *Those who manage technological change must often serve as both*
> *technical developers and implementers. As a rule, one organisation*
> *develops the technology and then hands it off to users, who are less*
> *technically skilled but quite knowledgeable about their own areas of*
> *application.*

Although their focus is that of technological change what they argue here is also true of almost any change process and is certainly true of the TOC/TP change process. This imposes a responsibility for the implementer to design the changeover in such a way that it is almost invisible. When people are transferring the TOC/TP knowledge into their own environment it is vital to ensure that the others within the organisation are ready to accept the new approach without question. There is also a major question here for the TOC/TP developer and educator. If they are to be successful then they must also be able to integrate the needs of both parties. For Leonard-Barton and Kraus (1985) the way forward is through a marketing approach. They argue that the

> *Adoption of a marketing perspective encourages implementation*
> *managers to seek to use involvement in the*
>
> *(1) early identification and enhancement of the fit between a product*
> *   and user needs*
> *(2) preparation of the user organisation to receive the innovation*
> *(3) shifting of 'ownership' of the innovation to users.*

The time given to achieving the buy-in of the other members of the organisation is felt to be a prime factor in the success, or otherwise, of the process.

Managing the introduction of change

Wooldridge (1982) notes the concerns of managers facing the introduction of change by saying

> ... the prospect of introducing technological change has brought about increasing despair amongst line managers. They cannot believe it when faced with outright opposition to change from employees and their unions, even when that change is blatantly vital to the survival of their organisation.

One of the major problems facing anyone concerned with this is that the reality of the situation is both complex and subtle. Again Leonard-Barton and Kraus (1985), who argue that the marketing approach will assist in the change process, have found that many implementations fail because 'someone underestimated the scope of importance of such preparation'. Leonard-Barton and Kraus scorn the idea that the technical superiority of the innovation will guarantee acceptance and that pouring abundant resources into the purchase and development of the technology at the expense of the implementation process will provide success. They propose 'not only heavy investment by developers early in the project but also a sustained level of investment in the resources of user organisations'.

Without proper implementation there is no improvement process and if the involvement of all the people concerned is not achieved then the likely outcome is not what might be expected. The whole point of the third question 'How to effect the change?' in the three questions of TOC/TP is to fully prepare the people for the change and indeed to involve them in that process. This is done through the surfacing of the obstacles that stand in the way of success and the raising of reservations, which refer to the possible negative outcomes of implementing the proposed solution. The notion of the marketing approach also implies that there are multiple markets within the organisation which require to be addressed. At each level of the company there needs to be a planned strategy, which applies at that level. Managers on one level will require a different response to managers or users at a different level. Leonard-Barton and Kraus believe that

> Top management and ultimate users have to buy into the innovation to make it succeed but marketing an idea to these two groups requires very different approaches... We believe the executive must view the new technology from the perspective of each group and plan an approach accordingly.

This buying-in to the proposed innovation leads to the concept of 'ownership' of the proposed change. Although the exact meaning will vary depending on the size and nature of the change project, the term implies the full involvement of all interested parties. Of course one set of difficulties not expressed here is when there is full buy-in from the people but not from the innovator, for reasons which will be examined later in this study. Of course any change of this nature involves a transfer from one set of technology to another. Therefore the identification of those who will influence the workforce is paramount. The opinion leaders within the organisation play a vital role at this stage. Equally important is the realisation that the opinion leaders may not be the actual managers within the departments, but others who, although they do not have the functional leadership, may have the *de facto* leadership.

The change agent

Whoever is responsible for the change, they all share one thing in common, they are agents for change. Atkinson (1985) notes the importance of the change agent when he writes that

> The key to change is recognising that a need to take action is an important aspect of the change process, and that a 'change agent' or 'catalyst' is imperative to the successful implementation of new technologies.

It is the nature of this person that is crucial to the success or otherwise of the implementation. Atkinson suggests the following description of the person who can deliver such change

> The individual, the catalyst who makes things happen, is central to effective implementation strategies. Whoever occupies this role must possess the requisite attitudes, skills, knowledge and experience to develop an objective overview of the problem, and create decisions, which work in the long term. This 'facilitator' must also be able to harmonise enthusiasm, grasp opportunities, explore the sources of resistance and change attitudes in order to promote a healthy and effective organisation ... change cannot create itself. It must be welcomed as an opportunity for those who work in the organisation to take some responsibility, and help prepare for, and create their own future.

Hersey and Blanchard (1988) picked up the theme of motivation and leadership, two key aspects of a successful change agent, when they described what makes a good leader. Through the development of situational leadership they sought to provide a 'common language to help solve performance problems'. They go on to suggest that their approach can be used to 'diagnose leadership problems, adapt behaviour to solve these problems and to communicate solutions'.

In their analysis of what they call a 'real change leader' (RCL), Katzenbach (1995) and his team consider the key elements or attributes of a successful change manager. He defines such major changes as

> ... *those situations in which corporate performance requires most people throughout the organisation to learn new behaviours and skills. These new skills must add up to a competitive advantage for the enterprise, allowing it to produce better and better performance in shorter and shorter time frames.*

He also describes the common characteristics of the RCL as

> *(1) commitment to a better way*
> *(2) courage to challenge existing power bases and norms*
> *(3) personal initiative to go beyond defined boundaries*
> *(4) motivation of themselves and others*
> *(5) caring about how people are treated and enabled to perform*
> *(6) staying undercover*
> *(7) a sense of humor about themselves and their situations.*

This leads to their definition of the term 'real change leader' as

> *Individuals who lead initiatives that influence dozens to hundreds of others to perform differently – and better – by applying multiple leadership and change approaches.*

Throughout his study Katzenbach uses cases to describe what kind of effect RCLs can have, in particular they go after 'specific performance improvements based on building new skills and attitudes, and getting commitment from all hands'.

The close relationship between what Katzenbach calls an RCL and a TOC/TP practitioner is not surprising. Both have a focus rooted in the market, both are working to a vision of what can be, and setting out to achieve it. Words that are part of the language of a TOC business analyst, known as a Jonah, such as enthusiasm, commitment and trust are also part of the RCL vocabulary. Katzenbach recognises the importance of vision in the process of change. He writes,

> *You have to start out with a vision that isn't well articulated. You have to sense that it can be grey, it can be murky, but it should have at least the attributes of things you want. Then I think it is helpful to talk long and hard to a lot of people.*

The next stage in the process is to determine whether the agent of change should come from inside the organisation or outside. In one sense, given the nature of this research and the role of the researcher, the answer to this question is both inside and out. The primary force for change is with the people attending the various programmes, however, the researcher in his or her role of educator is also influential in the change process. Atkinson (1985) considers both

> *Clearly there are many advantages associated with using personnel within the structure to bring about change. Organisational knowledge, relating to structure, organisational culture, departmental and work groups, managerial responsibility etc., is an important asset, which the internal change agent possesses. Unfortunately there are disadvantages regarding subjectivity, bias and dependence for future career and promotion prospects. These negative factors all tend to suggest that the internal agent for change is not sufficiently detached from the situation to perform his function with discretion.*

When considering the position of agents being external Atkinson argues that their advantages lie in areas such as

> *... skill attainment, experience of change programmes in different cultures and structures, objectivity etc. All this helps the external practitioner to take a detached and professional view. Unfortunately, external consultants take a great deal of time to become acquainted with organisational philosophy, policy and practice.*

Caruth (1974) in his examination of the systems analyst as a change agent noted that there are

> *... four areas of major concern to the systems analyst*
>
> *(1) basic human motivation*
> *(2) why people tend to resist change*
> *(3) the ways in which people resist change in the workplace*
> *(4) how to overcome resistance to change.*

Of the first area Caruth considers that this is a key area on which to focus. It is necessary for long-term improvement and change to reinforce the motivation of the workforce and that the 'greatest opportunities for motivation lie in the areas of egotistic and self-fulfilment needs'. It is often due to the lack of opportunities for most employees to use the creative side of their personality in their work and to a lack of recognition and appreciation that they become stagnant in their approach. Again Caruth makes the point that

> *There are areas in which management must concentrate its motivational efforts. These are the areas which the systems analyst should utilise in his efforts to bring about change with a minimum of disruption and resistance.*

Atkinson (1985) considers that the best approach centres on what he calls the team approach. This he describes as the

> ... *coming together and grouping of external specialists who possess expertise, skill and experience, coupled with the organisational strengths of the internal practitioner, helps bind the partners of change. The team approach develops a 'synergistic' learning climate where the experience, knowledge and creation of ideas can be maximised.*

Leonard-Barton and Kraus (1985) also considered the formation of the implementation team and argued that it should include

> *(1) a sponsor, usually a fairly high-level person who makes sure that the project receives financial and manpower resources and who is wise about the politics of the organisation*
> *(2) a champion, who is a salesperson, diplomat and problem solver for the innovation*
> *(3) a project manager, who overseas administrative details*
> *(4) an integrator, who manages conflicting priorities and moulds the group through communication skills.*

Resistance to change

For resisting change itself, Caruth (1974) puts forward the suggestion that there are a number of key factors. The first is that change, in any form, is perceived as a threat. 'It is seen as a source of frustration, an obstacle which prevents an individual from satisfying a basic need.' It is precisely this fact that is a function of one of the key hypotheses of this research. It is not so much that the need is not satisfied rather it is threatened.

Caruth continues to detail what he considers are more specific reasons, the first being economic security where the change is seen as threatening the source of income. Depersonalisation is a further cause for resistance to change, as Caruth puts it, '... if he feels that the change will carry with it the notion of powerlessness, loss of autonomy, or a loss of identity with the products of one's efforts'. Job status is a further causal factor where change could imply that some of the trappings associated with the present position might be swept away or reduced in status after the proposed change. Change is also seen as introducing levels of uncertainty about competence and the re-skilling, or worse de-skilling, which may result. All this produces a situation where change is seen as disruptive and also possibly a destructive force to the social group within the workplace and hence people tend to resist such change.

The methods used in such resistance can vary widely from the merely outspoken response to the quiet yet positive sabotage of the implementation. Caruth examines a number of possible methods of opposition, ranging from open aggression to the spreading of spurious rumours about the new implementation and the effect it will have on staff. Some will just withdraw and lend no support to the new changes, which in turn leads to the situation where there is no sense of involvement and responsibility shown towards the new system. Others will be totally negative expressing the opinion that the new system will never work and should never have been introduced in the first place. Finally, there is the point when the person withdraws totally and this will often lead either to the person being transferred to another department or even leaving the company altogether. Any implementation process that results in the kind of negative outcomes as described by Caruth is already a failure as it has resulted in lose–lose rather than win–win.

This situation is full of potential danger for the change agent as he, or she, has an interest in the success of the implementation. It is important therefore to overcome the barriers to change. Top of the list according to Caruth is that of communicating with the interested parties. If the people who are going to be affected by the change are directly involved with the change from the outset then they have a stake in the development of the system. The people in the organisation are important sources of information, often knowing the underlying methods of operation that exist in the company. It is important that this participation is honest. As Caruth explains

> *If participation is used simply to placate employees they will very quickly see through the ruse and resistance, perhaps more fiercely than ever, will soon develop.*

Hence when such change is being considered the management should consult with employees from the earliest point. Again Caruth states

> *Management should carefully explain the reasons for the change, how it will be implemented, what requirements the new system will impose, the benefits to employees etc.*

Caruth also emphasises that the negative as well as the positive aspects should be explained. In conclusion he writes,

> *People can be conditioned to accept change as a normal occurrence if rewards for acceptance are positive. People will seek out opportunities for change if the right climate has been created by management ... the majority of people will come to accept change if they are allowed to participate in developing the change, if management communicates openly with them concerning change, and if they are taught to accept change as a way of life.*

Leonard-Barton and Kraus (1985) also accept that resistance to change is a major factor and argue that there are two main types of resistance. These they define as firstly overt resistance, which forms as a function of mistakes, or issues that have been overlooked within the implementation plan and secondly tacit resistance, which is a function of underground feelings, which develop into action against the implementation.

The politics of change

The issue of power, the use of power in organisational contexts, and the problems that surround it have been researched and discussed by writers such as Handy (1985), Drucker (1980), Kakabadse and Parker (1984), Pfeffer (1981 and 1992), Lee and Lawrence (1985) and Morgan (1986). What is central to all of these commentators is the fundamental importance of recognising the political dimension associated with organisations and in particular that of change management. The individual who is tasked with managing the change process must recognise the power dimension of what he or she is doing and the likely impact it will have on themselves and others within the organisation.

The person tasked with change has to be aware of whatever power he or she has and be able to determine how this power might be properly used. Leonard-Barton and Kraus (1985) call this person the product champion who will nurture and attempt to anticipate opposition from the person they call the assassin who will equally try to destroy innovation. This the assassin can sometimes do with one careful shot, which means that the champions have to marshal their forces carefully. The most common reasons for this opposition are the fear of de-skilling, loss of power or lack of personal benefit. Leonard-Barton and Kraus feel that a good implementation plan should '... try to identify where a loss of power may occur so that managers can anticipate and possibly avert any problems arising from that loss'. Thus any innovation must offer an obvious advantage over the old system or there will be little incentive to use it. The implementers have considerable power at their fingertips, which can be seen in two primary aspects, positional power and personal power.

Leonard-Barton and Kraus also identify one more character, the hedger. These people sit on the fence waiting for signals that can give them some idea of which way the implementation is going. These people tend to avoid risk and can be found at any level within the organisation. The best way to counter their influence, according to Leonard-Barton and Kraus, is for those in charge of the implementation to send out the right signals so that the hedgers are in no doubt. This can take almost any form from a speech or presentation to a simple quiet word. It is also crucial that the managers at all levels are speaking the same words at the right time. Finally, Leonard-Barton and Kraus consider the important step to be that 'managers... bring the criteria used to judge the performance of the users of the innovation into conformance with the demands of the new technology'.

They conclude by saying that the task of converting hedgers is not an easy one to achieve but it is the most inescapable. Indeed

> *... as the competitive effects of new technologies become even more pronounced, the work of implementing those technologies will increasingly pose for managers a distinctive set of challenges – not least the task of creating organisations flexible enough to adjust, adapt and learn continuously.*

Power is a key feature of change programmes. Etzioni (1964) discusses the difference between position power and personal power, the distinction springing from his concept of power as the ability to induce or influence behaviour. Etzioni postulates that the best situation for a leader is when he or she has both personal and position power. It is then necessary to consider the use of this power as to whether it will result in success or effectiveness or both. Hersey and Blanchard (1972) consider this by saying,

> *Success has to do with how the individual or group behaves. On the other hand, effectiveness describes the internal state or predisposition of an individual or group and thus is attitudinal in nature. If an individual is interested only in success, he tends to emphasize his position power and uses close supervision. However if he is effective he will depend also on personal power and be characterised by more general supervision. Positional power tends to be delegated down from the organisation, while personal power is generated from below through follower acceptance.*

This leads Hersey and Blanchard to the conclusion that

> *... a manager could be successful, but ineffective, having only short-run influence over the behaviour of others. On the other hand if a manager is both successful and effective, his influence tends to lead to long-run productivity and organisational development.*

Change/implementation models and conflict resolution examined

Katz and Kahn (1978), like Checkland, developed their approach to organisations with a clear association with open systems theory. A key feature of their work is the careful definition of aspects such as cycles of input, throughput and output in a systems framework. They also recognise the different levels of systems and the interrelationships that exist within the system. It is precisely this relationship that is at the core of the effect–cause–effect logic of the TOC/TP. Through the connection of the logic the TOC/TP attempts to reveal the true causality that exists within the system, and thus the core problem. Katz and Kahn also recognise the importance of conflict and the dynamic outcome of such. They cite a number of potential sources of conflict, but offer little in the way of conflict resolution. They do suggest that 'conflicts can have both dysfunctional and functional consequences'.

Katz and Kahn go into the area of conflict in some detail, to them 'conflict requires direct resistance as well as a direct attempt and influence or injury'. Although focusing on conflict at an organisational level they do suggest that there are three commonly used concepts of conflict: conflict of interest, competition and conflict itself by which they imply incompatible interaction. This last concept of conflict is precisely the type of conflict most identified with this research. They go on to argue that '... every aspect of organisational life that creates order and co-ordination of effort must overcome other tendencies to action, and in that fact lies the potentiality for conflict'. With respect to change, they suggest that

> *Organisational change is necessary for survival, but an organisation with no internal resistance to change would be no organisation at all; it would move in any direction, and in response to any suggestion. Change and resistance to change, however, mean conflict.*

It is the recognition that conflict is inevitable that is so encouraging. While many people are trying to avoid conflict, they are actually trying to avoid what is natural in organisations. The key to the reality of conflict lies in the knowledge that the conflict can be used to good effect, much in the way that Follett (1995) suggested. This means that some form of conflict resolution is vital to on-going improvement and change.

Therefore the reason why many improvement programmes fail to achieve the expected targets and benefits claimed of them is the absence of a conflict resolution mechanism. These conflicts can occur at almost any point of an improvement process but are most prevalent at two key points. The first is when the core problem of the area under review has been identified and verbalised, and the second during implementation. These two points are part of any improvement process. In 1986, following some research completed at Leicester Polytechnic, I described such a process as comprising decision making–implementation–consolidation–expansion, shown in Fig. 2.2.

The process was assumed to proceed smoothly through each stage and, at the time, the research confirmed the importance of the first stage as being the most crucial to the final outcome. This first stage included the

| Decision making | Implementation | Consolidation | Expansion |

Fig. 2.2. Hutchin change model (1986)

basic decisions about what was required and the decision to go ahead made. Central to the ability to make the right decision were factors such as what must be done, which areas are the most important, and what level of investment is required. The implementation, which included any training that might be required and the necessary preparation within the organisation for the new systems being installed, followed this.

The third stage, consolidation, came once the initial implementation had been completed. At this point the system was either moving to a successful implementation or significant problems were being experienced. If these problems could not be overcome then the final stage, that of expansion, could not be reached. This stage was concerned with the growth of the new system within the organisation into new areas and perhaps beyond into other aspects of the organisation.

The final stage in this analysis of the literature is to consider what happens when changes have taken place. Every time a change is implemented in an organisation something can be learned. It may be from failure or from success, but either way there is an opportunity for learning to take place. This learning is vital if the organisation is to learn from mistakes, and to ensure that they are not made a second time. What is equally clear is that many organisations miss this opportunity.

Organisational learning

In the field of managing change, a key feature of successful change programmes is the way in which the organisation learns from what has happened. This may apply to either the individuals concerned on their own or collectively or to the organisation as a whole. Whichever is applicable, and it may be both, the opportunity to learn from the experience should not be missed.

Kolb, Rubin and McIntyre (1971) outlined such a learning model as shown in Fig. 2.3.

They observe that

> ... this learning cycle is continuously recurring in living human beings, Man continuously tests his concepts in experience and modifies them as a result of his observation of the experience. In a

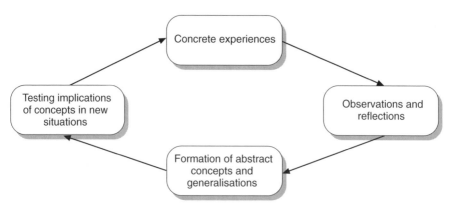

Fig. 2.3. Kolb learning cycle diagram

> *very important sense, all learning is re-learning and all education is re-education. Second the direction that learning takes is governed by one's needs and goals. We seek experiences that are related to our goals, interpret them in the light of our goals, and form concepts and test implications of these concepts that are relevant to our felt needs and goals. The implication of this fact is that the process of learning is erratic and inefficient when objectives are not clear.*

Checkland (1981) in his application of soft systems methodology (SSM) also considers the importance of learning. He argues that SSM is a learning system in itself. If the process is being used to address problems, in particular soft, fuzzy, unstructured problems then as far as Checkland is concerned that

> *... the methodology is a learning system, and in tackling unstructured problems, could only be a learning system, rather than a prescriptive tool, is due to the special nature of human activity systems.*

This raises the question of why people do what they do. Checkland argues that this is a function of the view the individual has of the world. Their actions are conditioned by their thinking. The interpretation of what is happening is also conditioned by this view of the world. Checkland uses the term 'Weltanschauung' to describe this, although he usually abbreviates it to 'W'. Checkland describes this in more detail when he writes

> *We attribute meaning to the observed activity by relating it to a larger image we supply from our minds. The observed activity is only meaningful to us, in fact, in terms of a particular image of the world or Weltanschauung, which in general we take for granted.*

This suggests that the W any one individual has determines actions. Another term for W is paradigm. For many years a particular paradigm may be appropriate for a particular set of circumstances. However, reality changes and with that change pressure is placed on the ruling paradigm, until it gives way to new thinking, a new paradigm. This is what Kuhn (1970) defines as 'paradigm shift'. Hence, given a set of problems, the way in which the problem is addressed is a function of the W or paradigm of the problem solver. If the solution is successful, the paradigm continues to be valid. If the solution is unsuccessful then the paradigm eventually faces a major challenge to the assumptions of validity that lie behind it.

Checkland observes this when he writes

> *It is characteristic of us that we cling tenaciously to the models which make what we observe meaningful. We celebrate Newton and Einstein as the very greatest scientists precisely because they forced the establishment of new Ws. Both were able to establish hypotheses which survived severe tests and hence became public knowledge, and were based on revolutionary frameworks, on Ws different from the prevailing ones of their time ... The Ws of an individual man will in fact change through time as a result of his experiences. And the Ws of a group of men perceiving the same thing will also be different. It is because of these two facts that there will be no single description of a 'real' human activity system, only a set of descriptions, which embody different Ws. In a certain sense, human activity systems do not exist; only perceptions of them exist, perceptions which are associated with specific Ws.*

For Checkland the power of SSM is in bringing about the ability to break out of one W and move to another.

An analysis of change control models

Within most systems the normal procedure is for some kind of input to the system to trigger, or lead to, an output of the same system. There is also usually some form of feedback to give a degree of control to the system, as shown in Fig. 2.4.

The control mechanism usually serves to regulate the input in line with the output in order to prevent the system moving to an out of control position. This model is a fairly standard description of such systems. It is equally applicable to human activity systems or to most other types of systems. It does have limitations, however, particularly when one important aspect of the system is the ability to learn and thus avoid errors in the future. This ability to learn is a necessary function if the ruling paradigm of the organisation requires changing at any time. This ability

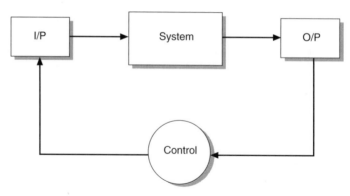

Fig. 2.4. Basic control model

to change paradigms has been discussed at great length by Argyris (1990, 1992, and 1993), Argyris and Schon (1996) and also by Argyris, Putnam and Smith (1985). They have developed a number of key concepts within the process of organisational learning.

These include the distinction between espoused theory and theory in action; the nature of single and double loop learning; and the relationship these all have for organisational learning.

The model developed by Argyris (1992) can be seen in Fig. 2.5. Argyris notes

> *Learning is defined as occurring under two conditions. First, learning occurs when an organisation achieves what it intended; that is, there is a match between its design for action and the actuality or outcome. Second, learning occurs when a mismatch between intentions and outcomes is identified and it is corrected; that is a mismatch is turned into a match.*

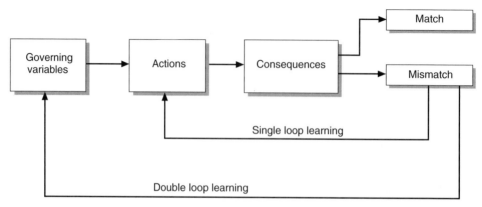

Fig. 2.5. Single/double loop learning

Referring to the models, Argyris defines them in the following way

> *Single loop learning occurs when matches are created, or when mis-matches are corrected by changing actions. Double loop learning occurs when mismatches are corrected by first examining and altering the governing variables and then the actions. Governing variables are the preferred states that individuals strive to 'satisfice' when they are acting.*

When change is necessary, Argyris suggests that single loop learning is very much in line with the model first introduced by Lewin (1947) comprising three stages, these being unfreezing, changing to a new pattern and then refreezing.

However, the model proved to be inadequate when change of a deeper nature was required. Thus the need for double loop learning is established. Argyris (1992) argues that

> *Such significant changes require changes in the organizational governing variables and master programs, that is double loop changes. But double loop changes cannot occur without unfreezing the models of organizational structures and processes now in good currency. These models, in turn, cannot be unfrozen without a model of a significantly different organizational state of affairs; otherwise, toward what is the organization to change?*

There is, however, an important aspect to what Argyris is saying here. The current model, although still working, is no longer valid. This implies that people are using an approach which they already know is not the one that is required. This leads to the distinction between espoused theory and theory in use.

Argyris (1992) argues that

> *One of the paradoxes of human behaviour, however, is that the master program people actually use is rarely the one they think they use. Ask people in an interview or questionnaire to articulate the rules they use to govern their actions, and they will give you what I call their 'espoused' theory of action. But observe these same people's behavior, and you will quickly see that this espoused theory has very little to do with how they actually behave. . . . When you observe people's behavior and try to come up with rules that would make sense of it, you discover a very different theory of action – what I call the individual's 'theory in use'. Put simply, people consistently act inconsistently, unaware of the contradiction between their espoused theory and their theory in use, between the way they think they are acting and the way they really act.*

At this point Argyris returns to the governing variables when he argues that

> ... *most theories in use rest on the same set of governing values. There seems to be a universal human tendency to design one's actions consistently according to four basic values*
>
> *(1) to remain in unilateral control*
> *(2) to maximize winning and minimize losing*
> *(3) to suppress negative feelings*
> *(4) to be as rational as possible – by which people mean defining clear objectives and evaluating their behavior in terms of whether or not they have achieved them.*
>
> *The purpose of all these values is to avoid embarrassment or threat, feeling vulnerable or incompetent. In this respect, the master program that most people use is profoundly defensive.*

This last element of Argyris is fundamental. If the change is of some significance then double loop learning is likely. If that is the case then the governing variables must also change. This is the same as the paradigm shift of Kuhn or the change in W of Checkland. However, Argyris suggests that at this point the whole approach of the individual becomes negative. If at the same time they are also aware of the conflict between the espoused theory and the theory in use individuals can now find themself in a degree of difficulty. They have to make decisions about change and whether they are prepared to take that challenge.

Conclusions

This chapter has set the scene for this research in terms of what has already been studied and researched. The key elements include the need to solve problems in a way which removes them altogether, therefore the need is to deal with core problems and not symptoms. It recognises that such problem-solving tools must be robust in all environments and answer the three main questions of, What to change?, To what to change to? and finally How to effect the change? Change of this nature will involve the panoply of change management issues, all of which must be addressed if success is to be the outcome. Finally there are the questions of how the individual faces up to the challenge of change for either him or her, and for the organisation. This final element implies the ability of the organisation to learn from what it is doing, to challenge the basic assumptions that govern the way it is managed and to be ready to change where appropriate. Contained within this final stage is the recognition that the differences between espoused theories of action and theories in use may also be driven by the measures that exist within the organisation at the time. Measures determine action, they determine the decisions that are made, and if they are also erroneous then people are already aware of the dichotomy that exists.

In terms of the research question raised earlier little has been said about the need to change the ruling paradigm of the individual. Argyris notes the importance of the governing variables but does not offer any mechanism to either describe the potential barrier or to determine the impact it might have. Checkland notes the power of 'W' but does not explore the impact it might have on the ability of the individual to change them. Although there is a wealth of knowledge about the process of problem solving, managing change and developing the learning organisation there is little within the literature to give guidance about the research problem.

CHAPTER THREE
The research question defined

Introduction

The research area, first introduced in chapter 1, raised the question of why do so many improvement projects fail. Why do people who have a robust solution they have developed still fail to implement it? Is there an obstacle to the process of change that so many improvement projects demand, an obstacle as yet undefined?

The previous chapter explored current thinking contained within the literature to determine whether this obstacle had already been described. Although some came close the area remained unclear and required further examination. This chapter lays out the research area in more detail, and develops the problem area of chapter 1 into the research questions, which lay at the heart of the research. This chapter will also set the boundaries for the research thus allowing for both focus and objectivity.

As noted earlier, while many companies are embarking on improvement projects many do not achieve the expected levels of results from their efforts. This is particularly true when the improvement involves significant change. This lack of results gives rise to greater concern when the people in the organisation use a detailed, logic-based approach whose whole emphasis is on ensuring successful change. Although this raises the question why this is so, it should be noted that not all failed and there were successes. Many had success in implementing the changes required in order to gain performance improvement. They felt no conflict either with others or with themselves. They simply did it. Others, however, did not achieve what was expected. They all went through the same process, often at the same time, in the same class. So why did some fail? This was the starting question of the research. It wasn't that they did not know what to do, they often had a clear and implementable plan to follow. In some way they were blocked.

This chapter therefore brings together the research questions first introduced in chapter 1 and the questions raised in chapter 2 from the analysis of the current literature. The intention here is to pull these two strands into one coherent structure which formed the basis for the research, developing the research questions more fully and then determining the hypotheses that lay at the heart of the research.

Selltiz *et al.* (1966) suggest that 'the purpose of research is to discover answers to questions through the application of scientific procedures'. In particular the questions being asked here are of an exploratory nature, exploring the variables that surround the use of problem solving and change processes, in this case the Theory of Constraints, in the pursuit of a successful implementation. Questions within this area of research are more concerned with issues such as 'what', 'who' or 'where'.

Again Selltiz *et al.* (1966)

> *In order to be answerable by research, questions must have one characteristic in common: They must be such that observation or experimentation in the natural world (including, in the case of the social sciences, the behaviour of human beings) can provide the needed information.*

They then go on to remind the researcher that

> *This does not mean that research will always emerge with an answer, let alone a definitive answer. Research is oriented towards seeking answers, but it may or may not find them. Characteristically, modern science, and especially social science, is an unfinished business.*

When considering the nature of inquiry they suggest that

> *Scientific inquiry is an undertaking geared to the solution of problems. The first step in the formulation of research is to make the problem concrete and explicit.*

They then continue by arguing that 'the first step in formulating is the discovery of a problem in need of solution'. Given the rigorous nature of the TOC/TP and the use of cause–effect logical structures, this grounding in a scientific approach had important implications for the robustness of the research and the findings. The TOC has at its core a clear determination to rigorously analyse problems and develop solutions.

As noted above, the research has at its core the TOC/TP and at the core of the TOC/TP lies the ability to determine causal relationships. Thus the whole approach is about the effect–cause–effect relationships that exist in all organisations. In recent years the terms cause and effect have given way to a *cause* becoming a change in an independent variable, and an *effect* to mean a change in a dependent variable. The connection between the cause and effect now becomes a functional relationship. Throughout the book the terms cause and effect will dominate, although at times I will use the more recent description.

43

Skinner (1953) when discussing functional analysis, writes

> *The external variables of which behaviour is a function provides for what may be called a causal or functional analysis. We undertake to predict and control the behaviour of the individual organism. This is our 'dependent variable' – the effect for which we are to find the cause. Our 'independent variable' – the causes of the behaviour – are the external conditions of which behaviour is a function. Relationships between the two – the 'cause and effect relationships' in behaviour are the laws of a science.*

Determining the research question to be answered

Given that research is setting out to determine answers, it is essential then that the problem, or set of problems, be clearly defined. Indeed without a clear formulation of the problem any solution that might be determined is likely to be of little value whatsoever. Thus if the nature of scientific inquiry is geared to the solution of problems the time spent in determining the problem is not wasted. The need for the problem to be both concrete and explicit is clear. It should also be noted that any such problem defined in this way is also in need of solution. This has roots in the approach of those pursuing chaos theory with the notion of sensitive dependence on initial condition. If the initial condition is not rigorously defined then any solution is likely to fail to deliver the expected results. (For a comprehensive discussion see David Ruelle 1991.)

Kerlinger (1973) recognised the importance of clear definition of the problem and the dangers of not doing so when he argued

> *It is not always possible for a researcher to formulate his problem simply, clearly, and completely. He may often have only a rather general, diffuse, even confused notion of the problem. This is in the nature of the complexity of scientific research. It may even take an investigator years of exploration, thought and research before he can clearly say what questions he has been seeking answers to. Nevertheless, adequate statement of the research problem is one of the most important aspects of research.*

Kerlinger describes three key aspects of defining the problem statement. The first is the question of relationship: What is the relationship between two or more variables contained within the problem area? The second refers to the way in which the problem has been stated, is it clear, unambiguous and stated as a question? The third element that Kerlinger suggests is vital is that of the ability to empirically test what is being studied.

Given that the problem, or set of problems, is both concrete and explicit, the next step is to consider a solution, or range of solutions to these problems. This leads naturally to the creation of hypotheses. The role of hypotheses in research is to propose explanations for certain effects and to gain guidance in the investigation of others. This argues that if the intention is to take a step forward then it is necessary to start with a suggested solution to the problem that initiated the inquiry. These potential solutions might be drawn from the area under review itself often in association with previous knowledge. When they are formulated in this way they are deemed to be hypotheses. Thus the function of hypotheses is to direct the research and develop the ability to determine order among the various effects being noted. The solutions formulated in the hypotheses may or may not be solutions; the answer to that question is the task of the research itself.

Kerlinger defines the hypothesis as a 'conjectural statement of the relation between two or more variables'. For Kerlinger, the important aspects of hypotheses are that they are 'statements about the relations between two variables'. Equally they also 'carry clear implications for testing the stated relations'.

One aspect of this research is the importance of causality, which has been introduced earlier. A hypothesis can assert that a particular characteristic or occurrence is one factor in the determination of another. This is called a hypothesis of causal relationship. The hypothesis acts as a guide to the kind of data that must be collected in order to answer the research question, it also assists in the way in which the data can be organised efficiently in the analysis. Kerlinger argues that there are two major elements of the power contained within hypotheses. The first is related to the ability to use hypotheses to achieve dependable knowledge. Given that the starting point for any research study is an observable phenomenon, which in turn leads to speculation about causes, Kerlinger argues that

> Scientists insist upon subjecting explanations of phenomena to controlled empirical test. In order to do this, they formulate the explanations in the form of theories and hypotheses. In fact the explanations are hypotheses. Scientists simply discipline the business by writing systematic and testable hypotheses.

He then goes on to argue that the power of hypotheses extends into the area of prediction. Finally, he suggests that there is little lost even when the hypothesis is not confirmed. He writes,

> Negative findings are sometimes as important as positive ones, since they cut down the total universe of ignorance and sometimes point up fruitful further hypotheses and lines of investigation. But the

> *scientist cannot tell positive from negative evidence unless he uses*
> *hypotheses.*

Thus the process is as follows, there is a problem and the problem is clearly defined, the problem space is formulated. There is also a desire to find a solution to the problem. There is already within the problem a suggested solution or explanation, which is rooted in our current intuition and knowledge.

Determining the nature of the research question

There are some obvious questions of a general nature that might form the starting point for the development of the research questions themselves. The inability to change is a function of the level of the change required. Given that there are differing levels of change, the hardest and most difficult is when the individual has to change a paradigm, a deeply held belief or value. This level of change can only be done by the individual. But how to cause such change? Even when the process for change has been used properly there are still many who refuse to do just that. The evidence for such a change can be overwhelming, they can even accept openly that such a change is beneficial to the organisation, and to themselves, and still they do not change. Why? There are many people who seem to prefer conflict without resolution. Why? There are many that continue to use conflict rather than deal with the core problem, even when it has been identified clearly and without reservation. This can even continue when they know not only what the core problem is but also the impact it is having on them, others within the organisation, and the organisation itself. Why?

Perhaps a process that offers a solution to a core problem, which involves changing a deeply held belief, changing a core paradigm, will be seen as a threat. If the intention within companies is to be able to develop and maintain a process of on-going improvement, it is clear from a great deal of current research that many managers do not know how to achieve this. The biggest constraint to improvement is the manager. Part of the knowledge gap is that there are few mechanisms to allow people to understand their role in the non-performance of their department or area of responsibility.

From this mix of problems the following questions were seen as encapsulating the issues raised above. Given the rigour of the process being used in terms of both problem solving and change management, why do some people fail while others succeed? Why do some people fail to deal with their core problems, which are directly under their control? Why do some people fail to deal with core problems when the process of analysis points sufficiently to what should be changed? Why do some people fail to deal with core problems even when it is hurting them and the organisations? Why do some people avoid taking responsibility for the area under their control – even if the process reveals their contribution to the current set of problems, either in terms of the creation of the problem or the continued existence of the problem?

The research was very much about exploring a phenomenon. It was about the development of a theory. A theory explains why, it is all about causality. It is also about stating what needs to be done to change whatever requires changing, and it is about the ability to predict behaviour. Therefore the research set out to both explore and to develop a theory. This is due to the nature of theories and their ability to provide an explanation, the ability to answer the question 'why?'. The theory attempts to explain why a phenomenon exists, and then hopefully leads to a statement of what needs to done to address the phenomenon.

The research questions to be addressed were as follows

- Can the block to improvement, which is by definition dysfunctional, be identified?
- Can the block be verbalised in a clear and logical fashion in such a way that allows for a proper analysis of the block?
- Is it possible to verbalise the block in such a way that it is possible to determine the necessary actions that must be taken in order to remove the block?

There are, as a result of the successful conclusion to the research, three further questions which can be addressed within this book. The first is, what are the necessary features of a solution to successfully overcome the block identified within the research process? Next, how effective are the features in achieving the objectives? and, finally, are there additional features which are more specific in nature rather than the generic features identified?

The explanatory phase – developing the hypotheses

Kerlinger argues that 'a problem cannot be scientifically solved unless it is reduced to hypotheses form, because a problem is a question, usually of a broad nature, and it is not directly testable'. However, there is also a requirement that the research allows for the development of a method which meets three basic criteria, these being: simplicity, generalisability and accuracy. Stuart (1983) has highlighted this problem when he considers that,

. . . we would all prefer

- *generalisability to specificity*

- *simplicity to complexity*
- *accuracy to approximation or inaccuracy.*

In the real world we face the dilemma that only two of these desirable qualities are obtainable at any one time.

Kerlinger (1973) also recognises this dilemma when he states in a similar fashion to Stuart,

At any rate, some kind of compromise must be made between generality and specificity. The ability effectively to make such compromises is a function partly of experience and partly of critical study of research problems.

The area of interest within this research is that which refers to the apparently dysfunctional and irrational behaviour of managers tasked with change. Questions abound such as, what kind of obstacle is this that prevents the implementation of a solution of such importance? Can this obstacle be defined, described, verbalised?

It is part of the hypotheses of the research that the individual is locked into his or her current, dominant paradigm. There are two stages to this. The first relates to the ability to verbalise this lock in the form of a conflict. This would allow the use of the conflict cloud technique to not only describe the conflict but also to surface the assumptions held by the person which lock him or her into the paradigm. It may be that the person is afraid of the change so that they do not know how to break free from this conflict.

The scenario for evaluating this is therefore to examine the area of failure and to determine whether the cause for the failure is either functional, that is part of the normal process and dealt with properly by the process of change, or dysfunctional. The assumption of the research is that dysfunctional failure, in combination with the existence of the obstacle of the paradigm lock, leads to observable conflict. Through the use of the cloud technique it is possible to describe this conflict. If there are sufficient examples of this then it should be possible to develop a generic cloud out of the collected data. The test of the hypotheses comes in at this point in order to ascertain whether the generic cloud is indeed the representation of the obstacle, the paradigm lock.

The next stage was to invite colleagues to test the cloud in their own environments. This in turn gives, if proved correct, greater confidence in the existence and description of the obstacle. Finally, the last stage was to postulate what options are open to deal with this obstacle and to test if possible. For the purposes of the research, this final stage was not seen as vital, only pointing the way forward. For the purposes of this book more time has been given to this thorny problem with some firm ideas about the way forward.

The hypotheses were as follows

- That there is an obstacle to change related to the existing, ruling paradigm of the individual and his or her ability to change that paradigm.
- That the tool of the TOC/TP known as evaporating cloud can verbalise this obstacle in a clear manner which also allows for the surfacing of assumptions that lock the individual into their current paradigm.

It is considered that this paradigm governs the decision-making process. This is particularly the case when the change affects them personally. This is very much in line with the 'W' of Checkland (1981) and the 'governing variables' of Argyris (1993). The research did not extend to the psychological development of values, beliefs and paradigms. For the purposes of the research, it was sufficient to acknowledge that those taking part had basic paradigms about who they were and what they were. Education, training and experience govern other paradigms, the rules by which people operate or manage within organisations. The psychological dimension of the research is forming the basis for further research and the development of new approaches within organisational behaviour.

The starting point for the research was the driving force for change, which was in conflict with the ruling paradigm thus creating the lock, and therefore the cause of the inability to implement the changes required. The framework for the obstacle was therefore proposed as being

(1) Change is required to deal with a major problem.
(2) The change is perceived as a threat to the ruling paradigm of the individual.
(3) The threat, and the conflict it contains, can be properly described through the use of the cloud technique.
(4) The cloud, through the surfacing of assumptions, gives direction to the way forward.
(5) Once the way forward has been determined there is a responsibility placed upon the individual to deliver, by implementing the original change.

CHAPTER FOUR

Organisational analysis

Introduction

The research problem first introduced in chapter 1 and the research questions developed in chapter 3 formed the foundation for the research. They also gave direction to the application of the appropriate method for gathering and analysing data. The focus of the research was the way in which people make decisions related to change. In order to understand the environment in which that activity takes place it is important to have a clear picture of that environment and the forces that affect the decision-making process. The answers being sought are very much related to the question 'why?'. Therefore the research process had to be capable of both capturing and explaining the data.

This chapter discusses the methods adopted and provides justification for the methods so chosen. These include the use of qualitative research methods such as case studies, participant observation and action research, and the importance of causality.

The starting point for most research is the recognition that a problem exists, or that there is a question to be answered. This may be driven by the researcher or by a client of some sort who approaches the researcher for assistance. The process of carrying out such research usually follows much the same path. Bennett (1983) describes the path as working through stages including literature review, possibly a pilot study and then the construction of a conceptual framework in order to develop a hypothesis. He then outlines the remaining steps as being testing the hypothesis, evaluation of the hypothesis leading to some form of interpretation of the results, the drawing of conclusions and making recommendations where appropriate. The final steps involve some form of report and, where necessary, action, or actions, taken.

This broad overview is then broken down into the component parts where the actual implementation of the research process is determined. Given that research begins with a problem, or a question to be answered, or both, the actual processes used must be in line with this requirement. Linked to this necessary condition, the questions of access to the data source, the nature of the hypothesis and the position of the researcher must all be considered. The research problem and the questions it raised were dealt with in the last chapter. From that starting position the research required an analysis over time of what people were doing which in turn lent itself to the use of case studies which then determined the data collection and analysis process. The collection of the data also involved the active involvement of the researcher, which implied a form of partici-pant observation linked to the whole concept of action science research.

Bouchard (1976) argues that

> The key to good research lies not in choosing the right method, but rather in asking the right question and picking the most powerful method for answering that particular question. Methods are neither good nor bad, but rather more or less useful for answering particular questions at a particular time and place.

Bennett (1983) defines management research as 'a systematic careful enquiry with anything to do with management'. In considering the research process he goes on to argue that it

> ... usually starts with a problem or question. The problem/question may be the researchers – they may wish to know which learning theory best explains different levels of performance in different situations. The problem may equally be initiated by the manager who wants to decide on the best technique for developing greater participation. In either case the requirement is for some information that will shed light on the problem and help make a decision to solve it. It may be that solutions are not the result of the research: an out-come might be the development of a new theory or body of knowl-edge. Whatever the result, the starting point is represented by an urge to find out, to explore, to evaluate – in short, to do research.

For Bennett research is

> ... concerned both with 'truth' and 'usefulness'. Some research – the theory-oriented – seeks often what is true, to find out exactly what the 'facts' are and, through a process of trying to refute the theory which explains these facts, present the real state of knowledge.

Kerlinger (1973) supports this view when he describes the method of science as a process for knowing and goes on to state that

> The scientific method has a characteristic that no other method of obtaining knowledge has: self correction. There are built-in checks all along the way to scientific knowledge. These checks are so conceived and used that they control and verify scientific activities

and conclusions to the end of attaining dependable knowledge. Even if a hypothesis seems to be supported in an experiment, the scientist will test alternative plausible hypotheses that, if also supported, may cast doubt on the first hypothesis. Scientists do not accept statements as true, even though the evidence at first looks promising. They insist upon testing them. They also insist that any testing procedure be open to public examination.

This is very much in line with the aims of this research. Not only must the approach deliver verifiable results; they must be capable of test and replicability. On proposing that the 'basic aim of science is theory', Kerlinger claims that science sets out to explain what is happening, the explanation being termed a theory. This he defines as a 'set of interrelated constructs (concepts), definitions, and propositions that present a systematic view of phenomena by specifying relations among variables, with the purpose of explaining and predicting phenomena'.

Another to argue strongly for the scientific approach was Skinner (1953) when he stated that

... science is not concerned with just 'getting the facts' after which one may act with greater wisdom in an unscientific manner. Science supplies its own wisdom. It leads to a new conception of a subject matter, a new way of thinking about that part of the world to which it has addressed itself.

He goes on to state that

Science is more than the mere description of events as they occur. It is an attempt to discover order, to show that certain events stand in lawful relation to other events. ... Science not only describes, it predicts. It deals not only with the past but with the future.

This whole passage from Skinner has important implications for the research that lay behind this book, and the process used. The TOC/TP grew out of a scientific background, the physicists search for knowledge and understanding. Here the focus of analysis is that of organisations and the people who work within them, but the intention is the same. Through the application of a rigorous, logical, analytical process, the bonds of cause and effect within organisations can be described and used in prediction. The ability to determine proper causal relationships between effects visible in organisations opens up a new dimension to the studies of organisational behaviour, development and psychology.

Skinner (1953) argues that

Science is first of all a set of attitudes. It is a disposition to deal with the facts rather than what someone has said about them.

The application of the scientific approach brings certain necessary conditions. Skinner notes that

> *Science rejects even its own authorities when they interfere with the observation of nature. Science is a willingness to accept facts even when they are opposed to wishes.*

This is not an easy concept to accept. Many people seek to find confirmation of their own paradigms and prejudices and often take great umbrage when such confirmation is not forthcoming.

Skinner reinforces this point when he argues

> *It is a characteristic of science that any lack of honesty quickly brings disaster. Consider for example, a scientist who conducts research to test a theory for which he is already well known. The result may confirm his theory, contradict it, or leave it in doubt. In spite of any inclination to the contrary, he must report a contradiction just as readily as a confirmation.*

The risks of not doing so are both high and damaging. Within any approach purporting to be scientific, it is this aspect which dominates. When the bonds of cause and effect are sought openly the result may not be what is expected, or perhaps desired, but it is the result. This aspect applied not only to the research, but also to the application of the TOC/TP itself.

Within the TOC process a high degree of importance is attached to the clear, precise verbalisation of the undesirable effects (UDEs) being analysed. As with any problem-solving approach there is a real danger that the individual can skew the analysis to meet his or her own particular needs. A common occurrence in terms of the undesirable effects is the statement that the problem, which is the cause of all the current UDEs, is the absence of the analyst's own preferred solution, the one he or she wishes to propose/implement/force upon you, the client.

If the TOC process lays claim to being a scientific approach, lays claim to high levels of rigour, lays claim to being a process of knowledge creation, then it must be robust enough, and sufficiently rooted in scientific method to give an honest and true answer to the question 'why?'.

Skinner (1953) echoes this when he writes

> *Scientists have simply found that being honest – with oneself as much as with others – is essential to progress. Experiments do not always come out as one expects, but the facts must stand and the expectations fall. The subject matter, not the scientist, knows best. The same practical consequences have created the scientific atmosphere in which statements are constantly subjected to check, where*

nothing is put above the precise description of the facts, and where the facts are accepted no matter how distasteful their momentary consequences.

Often in analysis using the TOC/TP approach the answer is not forthcoming. There is an insufficiency at some point in either the data set or the process as it is being used. It is vital not to try and force an answer at this stage. Skinner (1953) highlighted this when he argued

Scientists have also discussed the nature of remaining without an answer until a satisfactory one can be found. This is a difficult lesson. It takes considerable training to avoid premature conclusions, to refrain from making statements on insufficient evidence, and to avoid explanations which are pure invention.

Skinner (1953) concludes by arguing that science

... is a search for order, for uniformities, for lawful relations among the events in nature. It begins with, as we all begin, by observing single episodes, but it quickly passes on to general rules, to scientific law.

This was very much the focus of my research, to take each single episode, termed UDE, and through analysis devise some general principles related to the management of change, and perhaps determine some laws, which can stand the test of time.

The whole area under review, that of managing change, has been subjected to a vast amount of research over the years. It is an area where much is known. Yet still major problems exist in the management of change within almost all organisations. This suggests that while much is known, little has been successfully subjected to scientific rigour. The application of scientific method has been argued strongly by Skinner (1953) when he urged that this approach 'enables us to handle a subject matter more efficiently'. The intention here is to be in a position to predict the occurrence of an event. In so doing we are in a better position to be ready, we are more in control. When the subject matter is human behaviour, in organisations undergoing change, the ability to achieve this level of understanding is not a given. Skinner (1953) rightly states that

Behaviour is a difficult subject matter, not because it is inaccessible, but because it is extremely complex. Since it is a process, rather than a thing, it cannot be easily held still for observation. It is changing, fluid, evanescent, and for this reason it makes great technical demands upon the ingenuity and energy of the scientist.

The research being described here is primarily about people and the way in which they make decisions related to change. As noted above these decisions may be clear or fuzzy; they may be simple or complex. A key feature of the research was the ability to follow the progress made by those involved, to examine what they were doing and the success they were achieving. This led to the application of qualitative methods of research. This in turn set the initial context of the research as being exploratory, focusing on the research problem and questions developed in earlier chapters. Only once the exploratory phase was completed could the hypothesis be tested. The method used for the exploratory phase will be discussed later in this chapter.

The development of the research process – qualitative research

Robson and Foster (1989) considered that

> Qualitative Research is best used for problems requiring insight and understanding. It deals with explanatory concepts.

They define qualitative research in the following way

> The best definition of qualitative research is that it answers the question 'why?'. Through its inherent flexibility, its detailed and direct approach, it provides an explanation and an understanding of the consumer as an individual.

In terms of the research it was precisely the need to answer the questions in the previous chapters that started the whole study. Equally, given that the programmes that formed the basis for data collection were each different with different people and organisations, flexibility in approach was a fundamental requirement of the research process itself. Strauss and Corbin (1990) defined qualitative research as 'any kind of research that produces findings not arrived at by means of statistical procedures or other means of quantification'. They go on to suggest that 'it can refer to research about people's lives, stories, behaviour, but also about organisational functioning, social movements, or interactional skills'. Strauss and Corbin consider that the qualitative approach is an important means to uncover the true nature, and causality, of what people do. The researcher therefore has to 'step back and critically analyse situations, recognise and avoid bias, obtain valid and reliable data, and to think abstractly'. They continue to argue that qualitative research can be used to 'uncover and understand what lies behind any phenomenon about which little is yet known'.

Dey (1993) suggests that the emphasis of qualitative research is

> ... on generating theories rather than testing them. This reflects a concern with developing adequate conceptualisation of the social world before we develop elaborate theories.

He goes on to argue that

> ... we are often at the stage where the problem is to know what the problem is, not what the answer is. The qualitative analyst is cast in the role of a discoverer who unearths problems, identifies indicators and formulates hypotheses rather than investigating pre-determined problems within an established theoretical framework.

Within the work context, Cassell and Symon (1995) support these views when they state that

> ... qualitative methods are more appropriate to the kind of research questions we want to ask in our own work, that is: focusing on organisational processes as well as outcomes, and trying to understand both individual and group experiences of work.

They also highlight an important dimension of this research with respect to the position and involvement of the researcher when they argue that

> Because qualitative methods are frequently more interactive, more intensive and involve a longer-term commitment, researchers are more likely to build up a social relationship with the organisational members and therefore gain more insights into their collective understanding by actively sharing that experience.

This raises a fundamental aspect of the research. The ability to really understand what people were doing, and why, involved the development of trust between myself and the various students taking part in the research process. Recognising that I was also trying to learn and understand more about the process enhanced significantly the relationship and allowed for a free flow of information and critical comment. Research in organisations is fundamentally a practical endeavour and must be approached as such. It is vital to develop a genuine relationship with the subject though, at the same time, recognising that both might change as a result.

The use of case studies

Within the area of qualitative research the use of case studies is common. The research here focused on the experiences of the people taking part, and followed them over a six- to nine-month period. Throughout that time the researcher was involved in checking the process being used by the people.

Sommer and Sommer (1991) consider, in support of both Emery and Bouchard, that the

> *Case study is an in-depth investigation of a single instance. It can involve a unit as small as an individual or as large as an entire community or region. It provides the opportunity to apply a multi-method approach to a unique event or setting. Unlike other methods that tend to carve up a whole situation, community, or life into smaller parts, the case study tends to maintain the integrity of the whole with its myriad interrelationships.*

This final comment is particularly true of this research. If the obstacle is to be found it will be in its normal setting, organisations and organisational change. Sommer and Sommer also argue that

> *Another use of the Case Study is to test a theory. While a single exception is not sufficient for discrediting a theory, a supportive finding increases confidence in a theory's predictive power.*

Katz (1973, in Kerlinger) gives two broad categories of field study – the exploratory and explanatory or hypothesis testing. The former seeks to identify what is present now rather than predict relationships in the future. The three purposes, which are attributed to this category of field study, are

(1) to discover significant variables
(2) to discover relationships amongst them
(3) to lay the groundwork for more systematic and rigorous testing of hypotheses.

As these three purposes aligned with the needs of the research the case study approach was deemed the most suitable.

According to Kerlinger and Katz the advantages of field studies lie in the strength of realism, significance, variable action, theory orientation and heuristic quality. This also makes the point that the individuals who took part in the study were in familiar, known surroundings, thus reducing the level of disruption to their normal routine.

Emery (1967) favours the use of case studies, as they are a valid method for 'studying a problem by the detailed examination of the characteristics of single objects or events'. In arguing the case for the wider use of such studies Emery states that

> *... there is the overwhelming practical consideration that our scientific generalisations are called upon to help or explain problems to individual persons, families, work groups etc. These individual cases have to be studied in all their uniqueness if we are to decide what generalisations are appropriate and what action is to be taken in view of the particular condition of their existence. Secondly, there is also the dilemma in our research methods that the more the*

reliability of a survey is increased by taking more cases, the fewer the variables that can be studied for the same expenditure of research funds and time. Thus as a general research procedure, the case study has been used by many investigators to obtain detailed qualitative descriptions.

However, many researchers quoted by Emery, such as Paterson (1967 in Emery), have considered the case study to be of limited value suggesting that what can be learned from the case study alone concerns the case. Equally, Fensham and Hooper (1964) observed that the disadvantage of case studies is that they can never establish general laws or theories. Their strength, however, is that they can reveal important factors in complex social situations and generate powerful hypotheses. Emery (1967) considers these criticisms and offers the following insight

... the contribution of a single case will not (under any but perhaps experimental conditions) clinch an hypothesis; it will only add to its probability.

Bearing in mind the question of causality which lies at the heart of this research Emery then goes on to offer the following reason for supporting the case study approach

... the value of the case study method is not to be found in the process of adding but one more 'fairly typical' case to our statistical tables but rather in the selection of cases where we have reason to believe that the necessary and sufficient conditions for events may be most easily discovered or most easily verified.

When the question being researched involves the implementation of problem-solving approaches and the management of change, the case study approach is relevant. Emery (1967) argues that the case study can be used to serve many differing purposes including 'illustrations, to develop new hypotheses and concepts, to refine existing generalisations and to test hypotheses'. In the case of this research each of those have a place although the most important is that of hypothesis generation and testing. This research focus, with the identification of the various factors being a crucial element, meant that the ability to develop and test the hypothesis, which would allow for application to a wide range of organisations, was seen to be vital. Again, Emery feels that for the development of the hypothesis

... the case study is probably the most suitable method for opening a new field of study or for breaking new ground in a field wherein existing theory appears to have reached an impasse. By focusing the collection of information on a single, or small number of cases,

each piece of information will throw some light on, or be illuminated by, each other piece.

Emery goes on to consider what he feels are the two major results of such case studies. The first is that from the observations it will be possible to define concepts. Secondly, that it will be possible to postulate causal connections. Of course, to be able to justify the use of case studies is only part of the process; it is also necessary to ensure that proper procedures are followed. These include the normal scientific criteria of relevance, validity, reliability, consistency and comparability, all of which must be equally applied to case studies as to any other approach. This leads to the conclusion that any generalisations should be fully supported by the available evidence and also be defined with due consideration of that evidence. In addition, those factors that are reputed to be causal must be shown to exist and also to contribute to the interrelationships.

Field research of this type is also supported by Bouchard (1976) who argued that

... from the point of view of both science and society, field research is as important as laboratory research. This is because the field is where generality, applicability and utility of psychological knowledge are put to the test. The field researcher is the mediator of a relevant sociopsychological science.

Bouchard recognises the problems discussed by Emery above when he states that

... field researchers have not developed adequate intellectual justification for their role among their experimental or applied colleagues. The experimentalist disparages field research and calls for rigor, while the applied practitioner ridicules the sterility of the laboratory and calls for relevance. The field researcher finds himself hard put to meet one demand without sacrificing the other. Thus his dilemma.

Sommer and Sommer (1991) also suggest the requirements for a case study researcher as first proposed by Yin (1989). These include the ability to ask good questions, the ability to listen, to be adaptive and flexible in approach and capable of responding to the unexpected and see such perturbations as challenges and opportunities in the pursuit of knowledge. A good working grasp of the issues being studied is also a key aspect, as is the need to avoid bias.

Hartley (1995 in Cassell and Symon) considers case study research to consist of

... a dedicated investigation, often with data collected over a period of time, of one or more organisations, or groups within organisations

> with a view to providing an analysis of the context and processes involved in the phenomenon under study. The phenomenon is not isolated from its context (as in say, laboratory research) but is of interest precisely because it is in relation to its context.

Hartley goes on to suggest that

> The strength of case studies lies especially in their capacity to explore social processes as they unfold in organisations. By using multiple and often qualitative methods including observation, the researcher can learn much more about processes than is possible with other techniques such as surveys.... Case studies are also useful when it is important to understand those social processes in their organisational and environmental context. Behaviour may only be fully understandable in the context of the wider forces operating within the organisation, whether these are contemporary or historical.

She continues by arguing that case studies are

> ... tailor made for exploring new processes or behaviours or ones which are little understood. In this sense, case studies have an important function in generating hypotheses and building theory.

It is this final element that is of particular interest to this research.

Hartley concludes her analysis of the case study approach by arguing that 'the key feature of the case study approach is not method or data, but the emphasis on understanding processes as they occur in their context'. This is a fundamental aspect of this research. Without the contextual base of the TOC programmes and the working environment of the people attending, much of the potential richness of the data would be lost. It is, as Hartley argues, that 'case study research, because of the opportunity for open-ended inquiry, is able to draw on inductive methods of research which aims to build theory and generate hypotheses rather than primarily to test them'.

In order to develop the case studies I had to gain access to the right people who would provide the necessary data for the research itself. In this case the primary data sources were the programmes developed and delivered by myself and my colleagues. This meant that I was more than just watching the people in order to collect data, I was actively involved in the whole process. Therefore the case studies were collected through the active participation of myself, which takes the research method into the areas of participant observation and action research.

Data collection through participant observation

Waddington (Cassell and Symon 1995) describes participant observation as

> ... involving social interaction between the researcher and the informants in the milieu of the latter, the idea being to enable the researcher to study first hand the day to day experience and behaviour of subjects in particular situations and, if necessary, to talk to them about their feelings and interpretations.

Bouchard, quoting Hader and Lindemann (1976, in Bouchard), describes participant observation as

> ... based on the theory that the interpretation of an event can only be approximately correct when it is a composite of the two points of view, the outside and the inside. Thus the view of the person who was a participant in the event, whose wishes and interests were in some way involved, and the view of the person who was not a participant but only an observer, or analyst, coalesce in one full synthesis.

Bouchard argues that participant observation is often considered suspect but balances this by citing a significant number of classic studies in industrial and organisational psychology, which are based on this method. (Blau, 1967; Dalton, 1959).

Bouchard argues that there are a number of advantages in the use of participant observation. The first is that it 'focuses the researcher's attention on the behaviour of individuals rather than simply on their verbal interview or test-taking behaviour'. The second advantage is

> ... that it tends to force the researcher to look at the whole man, the whole organisation, and whole environment (social and physical) in an integrated way. Behaviour in the field doesn't make sense otherwise.

A third advantage proposed by Bouchard is that it 'puts him in the context of discovery and facilitates what Merton (1976, in Bouchard) calls the serendipity pattern of social research'. Bouchard then quotes Merton

> The serendipity pattern refers to the fairly common experience of observing an unanticipated, anomalous strategic datum which becomes the occasion for developing a new theory or extending an existing theory.

Participant observation is often described as occurring at four different levels. These are listed by Bouchard as being first, complete participant; second, participant as observer; third, observer as participant and fourth, complete observation. In the case of this research, the author was fully involved in the process, was completely open about the dual role, that of educator and researcher, and given the nature and rigour of the thinking process being used this was considered not to affect the outcome in any significant way. When using participant observation Bouchard argues strongly for the investigation to 'construct some sort of structure prior to entering the field or he will be overpowered'. It is the structure of the cloud technique discussed later that provides that insurance against the danger Bouchard describes. This plus the rigour contained within the whole set of TOC/TP tools. Had I tried to skew the analysis being undertaken it is clear from the logical rules that are central to the proper application of the TOC/TP that I would have failed.

One key issue discussed by Bouchard is that of objectivity

> *... a goal for which all researchers should strive, but one which is only approximated never achieved.*

He goes on to suggest a number of key factors in trying to achieve objectivity. These include the need to gather data from other sources, the need to separate facts from interpretation, the need to distinguish between informant and respondent data. There is also a need to be alert to the prejudices of the researcher and the possibility of bias in the interpretation of the data being collected. This same concern also applies to those taking part in the research process. It is important to examine both sides of the same equation, the ability to see the same situation from at least two perspectives. It is necessary to take note of changes in the attitudes, beliefs and emotions of the researcher, such changes often being clues to a lack of objectivity. It is equally important to recognise that the group taking part in the study are not a random aggregate but a social network who have been gathered together for a purpose. There is a danger in being over familiar and of getting too close to the group; linked to this is the need to ensure that they recognise the position of the researcher. Waddington (Cassell and Symon 1995) argues that the

> *... overall strategy is inductive rather than deductive, the participant observer uses his or her initial observation as the starting point from which to formulate single or multiple hypotheses. These hypotheses may subsequently be discarded or refined to take account of any unanticipated or contradictory observations which may emerge.*

Sommer and Sommer (1991) offer this when discussing participant observation

> *A Participant Observer has a defined and active role in what is happening, as distinct from being a spectator, bystander, or customer.*

They go on to argue that

> *Research through Participant Observation is a means of understanding the experience.*

As a result of my involvement in the research and the need to derive from the research positive outcomes of benefit to both myself and the student the study was also deemed to be rooted in the field of action research.

The application of the action research method

As the study set out to examine the process of change centred on the management of manufacturing companies, a key feature of the research was the ability to create knowledge which was usable. This meant that the study focused not only on developing knowledge that could be used in taking actions, but also contribute to the theory of action. Argyris *et al.* (1985) argued that such an action science could be used to 'articulate the features of a science that can generate knowledge that is useful, valid, descriptive of the world, and informative of how we might change it'. They go on to argue that

> *Leading social scientists distinguish action research from basic research by asserting that the intention of action research is to solve an important problem for a client and not necessarily to test features of a theory. ... We believe there is value in combining the study of practical problems with research that contributes to theory building and testing.*

Gummesson (1988) suggested that

> *A greater awareness of the possibility of carrying out research by means of qualitative methods and via the role of the management consultant ought to lead to improvements in the quality and usefulness of academic research in business administration.*

In their study of set-up reduction, Gilmore and Smith (1996) used the action research approach in order to find facts and carry out experiments with the aim of developing action solutions. It was chosen also for its ability to develop collaboration between researcher and the problem owners. They describe the action research process as following five stages, these being

(1) client perception of the problem
(2) client/researcher consult and contract
(3) data gathering and joint diagnosis
(4) feedback to the client group
(5) joint action planning.

For Gilmore and Smith, the main benefit was the 'participative nature of action research and the resulting extensive collaboration and employee involvement attained during the course of the exercise produced a sharing of knowledge'. Westwood (1995) also used the action research approach in his study of information systems for batch manufacture. The reasons for this stemmed from the goal, which was felt to be the development of new theory. He writes

> ... because we aimed to develop theory out of practice, we needed to collaborate with managers on the design process in an efficient way. The prescriptive approach evolved from earlier projects and enabled later projects to be conducted more swiftly. Fundamentally this was possible because the multi-site action research approach enabled us to focus the research question.

In the same way Grant (1996) described the action research methodology as following five stages, these being diagnosis, action plan, action taken, evaluation and learning. Once more the active participation of both researcher and client is seen as fundamental to the approach and to the outcome.

Clark (1972) in his study of organisational change compares five types of research, pure basic, basic objective, evaluation, applied and action. In examining action research he felt its strength lay in

> ... influencing the stock of knowledge of the sponsoring enterprise. In that sense it is a strategy for distributing knowledge.

He then goes on to adopt the definition first put forward by Rapoport (1970) for action research as being the ability to

> ... contribute to the practical concerns of people in an immediate problematic situation and to the goals of social science by joint collaboration within mutually acceptable ethical framework.

He then goes on to add that action research is

> ... a type of applied social research differing from other varieties in the immediacy of the researcher's involvement in the action process.

It is this very immediacy that is the determining factor in the use of action research in this study. As the programmes progress, the students are experiencing the generation of knowledge, which is of value to their company at the same time as learning about themselves. This is precisely the process that the research seeks to focus on. Clark considers that action research 'must possess an aspect of direct involvement in organisational change'.

Given the nature of the research, drawn from the programmes run by myself for people within manufacturing companies, it was clear from the outset that there were two key strands. The first concerned the ability of the individuals to address a major problem within their own organisation and the decision-making process associated with the problem. The second strand was the ability to examine closely the path that each individual followed and the methods adopted by them to deal with conflicts that arose out of the decision-making process. This second strand was seen as the key to the understanding of the research problem and the research questions described earlier.

Because of these two strands, it was felt that the research undertaken was clearly in the category of action research. Argyris *et al.* (1985) argue that this type of research

> ... *generates and tests propositions concerning (1) the variables embedded in the* status quo; *(2) the variables involved in changing the* status quo *and moving towards liberating alternatives; (3) the variables in a science of intervention that will be required if the previous propositions are ever to be tested; and finally (4) the research methodology that will make change possible and simultaneously produce knowledge that meets rigorous tests of disconfirmability.*

Within the research the importance of understanding the variables affecting the decision makers was recognised as fundamental to the exploratory phase. The first step in understanding what people did, and why, was to be able to verbalise their own environment in a clear and objective manner. It was vital that the current reality of the individual was clearly determined. This is very much in line with normal scientific research. Action science recognises the limitation of this approach in that first there is no focus on changing the current reality, and second, the picture developed will not include the defensive mechanisms that exist in order to maintain the *status quo*. This could be seen as a reason not to focus on current reality at all. However, this particular study set out to use current reality as the starting point for the process of change by surfacing these deeper conflicts over a period of time.

Argyris *et al.* (1985) suggest that

> *A corollary to the premise that the purpose of science is to describe reality is that generating knowledge about change is a second step, one that must wait until basic descriptive knowledge has been accumulated. In action science we agree that it is important to understand the world if we are to change it.*

It is important to recognise that in building the knowledge surrounding current reality; defensive mechanisms may be surfaced which can be seen as potentially threatening to the individual. However, these defences may lead to an inability on the part of the individual, and the organisation, to improve through learning and adapting. This inability could affect the ability of both to survive let alone flourish. Recognising the threat that surfacing such defensive mechanisms might pose to the individual was a key feature of this research, indeed it was precisely these mechanisms that offered the greatest insights to the obstacle to change and the conflict that surrounds it which lies at the heart of the hypotheses. What was vital to remember was that the research itself should not harm individuals or expose their weaknesses. Hence, in this research, it was clearly necessary to agree beforehand the limits to which both sides would go, either in open forum or in closed one-to-one sessions. Without the active collaboration of the individuals the research would not have been possible.

In considering action science, Argyris *et al.* (1985) quote Lewin

> *To proceed beyond the limitation of a given level of knowledge, the researcher, as a rule, has to break down methodological taboos which condemn as 'unscientific' or 'illogical' the very methods or concepts which later on prove to be basic for the next major progress.*

In this particular study I was fully involved with each person taking part. He was fully involved in working with people to deal with a major problem under their span of control. I was actively involved in teaching a set of logic-based problem-solving tools, in the analysis of the problem, the construction and validation of the solution, and the implementation. This placed me as an active participant with the problem owner while examining the process being followed. Action science also involves working on change experiments applied to real problems in social systems. The focus is on a particular problem, which the owner brings to the research and the intention is to deal with it. This in itself suggests an iterative process working round a cycle of problem analysis, implementation and review, and then repeating for each successive problem.

Action science argues that this will often involve re-education as the change process itself will involve the challenging of current paradigms related to thinking and taking action that may exist within the individual and the group. This re-education can only take place, however, if the problem owners themselves are involved in the activities of problem analysis, diagnosis and the choice of the action required to deal with the problem. This in itself suggests that action science challenges the *status quo*. In this way it can be argued that action science is, as proposed by Argyris *et al.* (1985),

> *... intended to contribute simultaneously to basic knowledge in social science and to social action in everyday life. High standards*

> for developing theory and empirically testing propositions organised
> by theory are not to be sacrificed, nor is the relation to practice to be
> lost.

The traditional approach to scientific research includes features such as
the ability to collect hard data, which can be validated by more than one
observer. Kerlinger (1973) defines scientific research as being a 'systematic, controlled, empirical, and critical investigation of natural phenomena
guided by theory and hypotheses about the presumed relations among
such phenomena'. He describes the approach, developed by Dewey, as
comprising the following stages: *problem–obstacle–idea* where the first
steps in understanding the problem are developed. He considers that it
is important to bring the problem into the open, to express the problem
in a way that can be understood and examined. This is followed by
hypothesis, a statement or proposition about the area under review and
the relationships that exist around it. The final step is that of *reasoning–
deduction*. There are a number of possible outcomes at this point, the
researcher may find that the original problem is not what the real matter
is about, that there are relationships previously not recognised, the
researcher may even find that the present analytical tools do not lead to
a solution. Kerlinger considers that the greatest area of importance is
the 'controlled rationality of scientific research as a process of reflective
inquiry, the interdependent nature of the parts of the process, and the
paramount importance of the problem and its statement'.

The 'evaporating cloud technique' for describing and analysing conflicts – a reminder

The research set out to use the cloud technique described earlier as the
primary analytical tool. This tool lent itself to opening doors of understanding. It is very much the gateway to knowledge in the sense that with a
simple conflict structure and then the surfacing of assumptions real, and
deep, understanding is possible about something that has hitherto
remained hidden from view.

The structure of the basic cloud, first introduced in chapter 1 (see Fig.
1.2) and repeated here, is shown in Fig. 4.1.

The main boxes, entitled **A**, **B**, **C**, **D** and **D'**, make up the main structure
of the cloud. The logic of the cloud is that of necessity. Thus **A** is the objective of the cloud and both **B** and **C** are the necessary conditions that are
required for the objective to be realised. These are defined as necessary
conditions but are not always sufficient in themselves for the existence
of the objective. In the same manner **D** is the necessary condition for **B**
and likewise **D'** for **C**. The conflict exists between **D** and **D'**. Once the

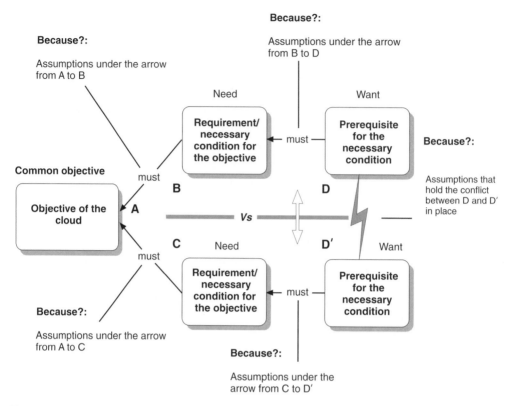

Fig. 4.1. The cloud diagram

cloud has been verbalised in this way the next stage is to ensure that the logic holds true by reading the cloud and amending the verbalisation where necessary. The cloud is read from the tip of the arrow to the tail. For example, 'In order to have (A) I must have (B); in order to have (A) I must have (C)'. The rest of the cloud is read in the same manner.

Once the verbalisation of the cloud is clear the next step is to surface the assumptions that lie beneath every arrow. This is done by adding the word 'because' after the phrases above. For example, 'in order to have (C) I must have (D') because...'. The assumptions that are surfaced are then placed in the appropriate box. The next step is to examine the assumptions to see which of them are erroneous and which are not. If an assumption is found to be erroneous then it may be possible to break the seemingly unbreakable conflict that exists. In this way the cloud is broken and the objective can be reached. This would then involve other tools of the TOC/TP.

A key element of this research is the hypothesis that the cloud technique can be used to determine and describe the conflicts that lie at the heart of the research. This would then allow for answers to the questions first raised in chapter 3. Once the data has been collected, this leads to the creation of explicit inferences which connect the data and theory. Within this study the hard data was essentially the conflicts which existed in the environment of each individual with respect to the change being proposed within their environment.

This is very much in line with Argyris *et al.* (1985) who argue that

> *The test of truth is rather that a community of investigators beginning with different assumptions and free to criticise any aspects of each other's work, converge on a set of beliefs. They can never be certain that their beliefs are true, but they can approach truth through a self-corrective process of rational criticism in a community of inquiry.*

Of course it is still possible to be wrong in terms of the analysis. It may be that the analysis developed is contrary to the existing paradigm(s) of the individual. If this is the case then the action taken by individuals becomes crucial to the successful outcome of their own improvement process. If they are capable of coping and implementing the new paradigm then potential conflict can be avoided. However, if there is no opportunity, no possibility for the individual to accept the new paradigm then the whole process is at risk.

Gummesson (1988) argues that

> *Paradigm is associated with revolutionary discoveries and changes in the natural sciences. Periods of normal science are superseded by paradigm shifts when established scientific norms are challenged. When our personal paradigm is attacked, we tend to feel threatened – our 'place to stand on' is being snatched away – and we tend to react by raising our defences rather than a frank appraisal of a new position.*

Popper (1992) has argued

> *To give a causal explanation of an event means to deduce a statement which describes it, using as premises of the deduction one or more universal laws, together with certain singular statements, the initial conditions.*

Argyris *et al.* (1985) support this when they state

> *The validity of proposed laws can be tested by deducing from them, in conjunction with certain initial conditions, descriptions of events that should be observed. Thus explanation and prediction are symmetrical, differing only with respect to whether the deduction is made before or after the observation of the event explained or predicted.*

The practice in any examination or analysis of this type is to carefully observe without preconception, and then to generalise from these observable events. The strength of the analysis is rooted in the honesty and purity of observation and the ability to validate the logic so constructed. In terms of this study and the hypothesis contained within it, Argyris *et al.* (1985) argue that

> *A proposal is tested by holding it responsible for the empirical impli-cation that can be deduced from it. If these implications do not cor-respond to what is actually observed then the theory... may be rejected. If a theory has no empirical implication, it cannot be tested, and it is for that reason not an acceptable scientific theory.*

Key features of the research were the elements of both passive observation and experimentation. The nature of the programmes that form the core of the data collection was, and still is, their focus on problem analysis and solution construction and implementation. Thus at two different levels, that of the students and their own specific problems, and myself as researcher and tutor, both are trying to predict what will occur and observe if the prediction is confirmed. Argyris *et al.* (1985) argue that

> *Experimentation is the most powerful methodology for testing theories because, by manipulating the initial conditions, the researcher can rule out alternative explanations.*

This focus on the whole process of problem solving from recognition to implementation ensures that this stage, implementation, is fully contained within the study. If problem solving and decision making are core parts then the implementation must also figure in particular when leading to results in terms of organisational performance. The success or otherwise of the solution is determined by the outcome of the implementation pro-cess and the measures used at that point. Although not always seen as a key element of such research Argyris *et al.* (1985) support the view that 'from the perspective of action science, implementation is not separable from crucial theoretical issues'.

The importance of causality

The importance of causality as part of a hypothesis is a key feature of this research. Selltiz *et al.* (1966) suggest that

> *A hypothesis of causal relationship asserts that a particular charac-teristic or occurrence (A) is one of the factors that determines another characteristic or occurrence (B).*

They continue by proposing that

> *Studies designed to test such hypotheses must provide data from which one can legitimately infer that X does or does not enter into the determination of Y.*

Research concerning causality therefore requires an understanding of the concept of causality. The usual way of considering causality tends to follow the line that a single event (the cause) always leads to another event (the effect) leading to the creation of effect–cause–effect relationships. Within science the emphasis is more usually with a multiplicity of determining conditions which together make any particular effect probable. Thus both common sense and scientific thinking are concerned with discovering necessary and sufficient conditions for any effect. Selltiz *et al.* suggest that

> *... while common sense leads one to expect that one factor may provide a complete explanation, the scientist rarely if ever expects to find a single factor or condition that is both necessary and sufficient to bring about an event. Rather he is interested in contributory conditions, contingent conditions, alternative conditions – all of which he will expect to find operating to make the occurrence of the event probable but not certain.*

Given that these conditions are seen as an important element of causality relationships it is necessary to define their meaning. A necessary condition is one that must occur if the effect of which it is the cause is to occur. If A is a necessary condition of B then B will never exist if A does not exist. For example, experimenting with cigarettes is a necessary condition for becoming addicted to smoking, as it would be impossible for the addiction to occur if the individual had never smoked.

A sufficient condition is one that is always followed by the effect of which it is the cause. If A is a sufficient condition of B then whenever A occurs, B will always occur. For example, should the optic nerve be damaged that is a sufficient condition for blindness as without the optic nerve it is impossible to see. There can also be situations where a condition may be both necessary and sufficient. This is described by Selltiz *et al.* as when

> *... Y would never occur unless X occurred and whenever X occurred, Y would also occur. In other words, there would be no instance in which either X or Y appeared alone.*

If the two examples described earlier are considered then neither fit this particular situation. Although addiction to smoking cannot happen without experimentation, there are some people who smoke who do not become addicted. It can therefore be stated that experimentation with smoking is a necessary but not sufficient condition of tobacco addiction. If addiction is to be fully understood it is necessary to find other contributory conditions. Equally, although damage to the optic nerve will lead to blindness it is not the only way in which sight can be lost. In this case the damage to the nerve is a sufficient but not necessary condition of blindness. In order to fully understand all the possible causes of blindness other conditions that lead to blindness have to be determined.

Selltiz *et al.* go on to argue that

> *A contributory condition is one that increases the likelihood that a given phenomenon will occur, but does not make it certain; this is because it is only one of a number of factors that together determine the occurrence of the phenomenon.*

What this is saying is that for any given effect, in this context, there is no single cause, but there has to be a second cause at least, which combines with the first cause in the form of a logical 'and' to lead to the existence of the effect. Without the second cause, the first is insufficient. This can be shown diagrammatically in Fig. 4.2.

It would be read in the following manner, 'if **A** AND if **B** then **C**'. At the simplest level the meaning is clear, that for **C** to exist both **A** and **B** must exist together. Using the example of smoking, research in this field is not satisfied that experimentation with smoking is a necessary condition for addiction, as it goes on to examine the effects of family, peer group and other factors that may be conducive to experimentation and which of these factors have a greater impact in the addiction element.

If it is possible to consider the concept that there can be a multiplicity of contributory causes, then it is equally valid to seek alternative conditions that may make the occurrence of the phenomenon more likely. This argues for the possibility of the logical 'or' connection which can be described as in Fig. 4.3.

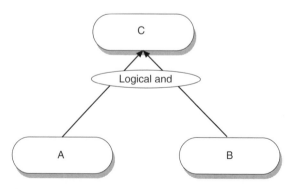

Fig. 4.2. The logical 'and' diagram

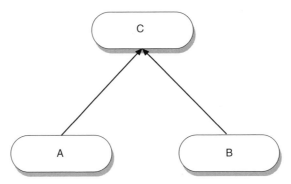

Fig. 4.3. The logical 'or' diagram

This would be read in the following manner, 'if **A** OR if **B** then **C**'. Now there is the need at this point to consider the relative weight of each of the alternative causes. The magnitude of the independent variable in this case **A** or **B** should be similar, thus leading to the even more likelihood of the dependent variable **C**. Where the magnitude is not equal, say in the ratio of 99:1 then the smaller of the two, although still a cause, can be considered insignificant. This may still apply when the ratio reached 80:20 depending on the nature of the causality.

Bearing in mind that there are two separate issues to contend with, these being described by Selltiz *et al.* as 'necessary but not sufficient' and 'sufficient but not necessary', it is important to make clear the distinction. Using an example of blindness, Selltiz *et al.* argue that 'the destruction of the optic nerve is a sufficient but not necessary condition for blindness, to understand all the causes of blindness we must seek alternative conditions that may produce it'.

This means that if there is a condition of 'necessary but not sufficient' there is a requirement to look for contributory conditions, i.e. there is insufficiency. Equally, if there is the condition of 'sufficient but not necessary' then there is a requirement to look for an alternative condition, in other words there is additionality.

However, it is also necessary to determine the environment in which the causality exists. Selltiz *et al.* suggest that

> *A factor that operates as a contributory condition of a phenomenon under a set of circumstances may not do so under another. The conditions under which a given variable is a contributory cause of a given phenomenon are called contingent conditions.*

These contingent conditions are therefore a function of the initial state in which the system resides. It is almost a fact of life – one that determines the impact of a contributory condition. However, to ignore or fail to

73

acknowledge contingent conditions can lead to misleading hypotheses, and once the notion of dependency on initial conditions is considered, the contingent conditions become much more important.

When considering the debate with respect to research Selltiz *et al.* argue that

> *Most hypotheses in social science are concerned with contributory or alternative conditions, and the contingencies under which they operate. However it is impossible to demonstrate directly that a given characteristic or occurrence X determines another characteristic or occurrence Y either by itself or in combination with other characteristics or occurrences (A, B, C, etc.). Rather we are always in the position of inferring from observed data that the hypothesis that X is a condition for the occurrence of Y is or is not tenable with some specified degree of confidence.*

This is arguing the case for postulating causality, if **A** then **B**, and then postulating a second effect, unrelated to **B** but caused by **A** which in turn confirms the original causality. The ability to predict an effect, find it and then to confirm the original causality can be seen in Fig. 4.4.

C is the predicted effect the existence of which confirms the existence of cause **A** and therefore makes the causality of **A** to **B** tenable. This is particularly useful when the cause being proposed is intangible. It is easy to fall into the trap of tautology. But if it is possible to predict an effect which must exist also as a result of the intangible cause **A** and if we can then find **C** our original causal relationship between **A** and **B** is made stronger. It might not yet satisfy the analyst but the pathway forward is not clear.

Of course identifying a contributory condition under certain contingent conditions may not be enough. Other possible contingent conditions must be examined to confirm the original hypothesis otherwise it is possible to

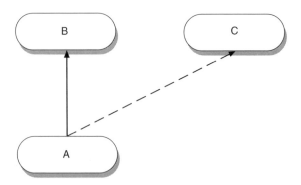

Fig. 4.4. Predicted effect diagram

make an incorrect inference. One such example is the question of the time order of events. Selltiz *et al.* describe it in the following manner

> *One event cannot be considered the 'cause' of another if it occurs after the other event. The occurrence of a causal factor may precede or may be simultaneous with the occurrence of an event; by definition an effect cannot be produced by an event that occurs only after the event has taken place.*

A further function related to evidence concerns concomitant variation. Selltiz *et al.* define this as 'the extent to which X and Y occur together, or vary together in the way predicted by the hypothesis'. They go on to argue

> *Evidence of concomitant variation, that is, that X (the assumed causal or independent variable) and Y (the assumed effect, or dependent, or criterion, variable) are associated in the way predicted by the hypothesis. In the case of a hypothesis that X is a contributory condition of Y, this would mean that Y should appear in more cases where X is present than in cases where X is absent.... Evidence that Y did not occur before X.... Evidence ruling out other factors as possible determining conditions of Y.*

When examining behaviour in the social sciences the use of an experimental model offers the best scenario. Selltiz *et al.* confirm this by arguing that 'when an experiment is possible it is the most effective method of testing a hypothesis that one variable, X, causally influences another variable, Y'. There are dangers, which must be recognised, however, and noted in constructing the research instrument. Given the nature of causality, and the nature of the variables involved, there is no way to be completely certain of the validity of the inferences being drawn. There is always the possibility that later research will reveal a new causality, or set of conditions, that were not taken into account in the original study. Einstein changed the description of the Newtonian world and Newtonian physics, but Newton could not have known what Einstein did and therefore can be excused and the limit of his theories properly recognised. Selltiz *et al.* recognise this aspect and suggest that

> *This possibility of fallacious inference makes it necessary to evaluate experimental findings in the context of other knowledge. Confidence in a research result requires not only statistical evidence of its reliability ... but, in addition, evidence that the interpretation is in keeping with other 'facts' about which one has confidence. This is why the establishment of confidence in the imputation of any causal relationship between events requires repetition of research and the relating of the findings to other research.*

Thus the requirements of such research become clearer. Selltiz *et al.* put it in the following manner

> *If one wishes to draw the inference that variable (X) is the 'cause' of another (Y) three types of evidences are necessary: (1) that X and Y vary together in the way predicted by the hypothesis; (2) that Y did not precede X in time; and (3) that other factors did not determine Y... In addition – and sometimes more important – the investigation must consider whether factors other than X may be the determinant of Y. In general this is done by introducing additional variables into the analysis and examining how the relationship between X and Y is affected by these further variables. If the relationship between X and Y persists even when other presumably relevant variables are introduced, the hypothesis that X is a cause of Y remains tenable.*

If changes take place then a contingent condition (Z) has also been identified for when the X–Y relationship holds true. This now leads to the need to determine three possible conditions

(1) when the relationship is spurious
(2) when the process has been traced by which X leads to Y
(3) when a contingent variable has been specified.

Conclusions

This chapter has introduced the primary methods used within the research to both gather and evaluate data. With respect to the first stage of the research, that of exploring the research questions, the use of the case study approach and the use of participant observation and action research, these have now been discussed as the main vehicles employed. The next chapter describes the actual collection of data and the development of the cloud technique for describing the data collected, and begins the process of analysis.

CHAPTER FIVE

Collecting the data

This chapter is concerned with the process of data collection and initial analysis. In chapter 1 the basic question of the research was first raised, namely the existence of an obstacle to successful implementation of change. The nature of the research therefore required access to a group of people who were seeking improvement in their organisation, in particular an improvement in the financial position.

During the period of the research, from 1993–1996, I was able to gain access to such a group of people. They all met the criteria set in the initial assumptions outlined in chapter 1. They were all involved in programmes in which I was also involved. These programmes were part of the education offered by the Avraham Y. Goldratt Institute in the UK and included programmes covering production, project management, sales and marketing, and strategic development. I was responsible for the presentation of the programmes and the follow-up activity inside their organisations. The overall timescale for these projects was typically between two to three years.

Overview of the 'Jonah Programme'

The primary programme attended by the main research group was entitled the 'Jonah Programme'. This is essentially an enterprise-wide analysis addressing issues of performance typically financial, with respect to the revenue chain of the organisation. Each organisation is described in the context of a revenue chain which links the supply base, right through the company, to the market. Each and every function or activity within the organisation is part of this chain, no element can be seen as a stand-alone entity, they are all linked. Thus only the optimal operation of the whole chain is of any importance, the local performance of any link being irrelevant in the context of business performance. The key is to determine the weakest link, the constraint, within the organisation, or its supply base, or indeed does the constraint lie in the market. The second dimension is to determine whether the constraint is physical or, as is more likely, a policy. This requires a rigorous process of effect–cause–effect. It is this process that is what the TOC/TP process is all about.

Therefore the process of analysis contained within the TOC/TP must follow a specific path. At the heart of the approach lies the intention of determining the core issues creating the many problems manifest within the organisation, and from that analysis to develop a breakthrough solution that is both implementable and addresses the problems once and for all. The results should include a substantial improvement in the bottom-line performance of the organisation, and a substantial reduction in the levels of stress and conflict.

The starting point for all such analyses is the recognition of a set of problems affecting the organisation's ability to achieve its goal. The manifestations of these problems are termed undesirable effects (UDEs). They are termed effects as the basic assumption of the TOC/TP is that there are fundamental causal relationships between the problems being experienced and their causes, to the extent that the number of causes is probably very small. If that cause can be determined by rigorous analysis then addressing the cause will always be more effective than addressing each effect in turn. The application of a scientific analysis to problems is not new, but the tools contained within the TOC/TP offer a degree of rigour not found elsewhere.

Once the UDEs have been presented they are subjected to scrutiny. There are various points throughout the TOC/TP process where scrutiny is applied but none more important than at the UDE stage. This is where the notion of sensitive dependence upon initial condition has the most impact. The developed solution depends entirely on the analysis carried out now. If the UDEs are not subjected to scrutiny they might not describe properly and fully the reality being examined. The UDE must be properly defined, it must comply with a set of criteria, it must be an accurate statement of the effect, it must be a single statement, not a combination of effects rolled into one for ease of communication. Once the UDE has passed this level of scrutiny if later in the process problems with the verbalisation occur the process itself will pull the individual back to this starting point for even further analysis of the UDE. The UDE should also be placed in its position within the revenue chain of the organisation, in the place where it has the most impact. There should also be, if possible, a financial measure determined. This assists, when looking at the whole picture, with determining the real impact the UDEs have upon the whole system.

The next stage is to construct the UDE clouds. These are described later in this chapter. Once they have been constructed for each UDE they can then be validated by the team and by myself as the tutor of the programme. Once they have passed this level of scrutiny they can then be considered ready for combination into a composite cloud. Each person attending the programme will choose three UDE clouds for this activity and construct the composite cloud. Once each person has done that the composite clouds will be combined into what should be a generic cloud for the organisation as a whole. At all times the scrutiny process continues and no cloud is allowed to pass to the next stage without such validation. The final stage of this element of the process is to construct the communication analysis. This allows for the communication of the analysis to date to be made to other members of the organisation. Once this has been constructed, validated and communicated it is possible that the first stage of the change process has been achieved – consensus on the nature and impact of the problem.

Through the surfacing of assumptions for the clouds it is possible to search for erroneous assumptions that will signal the pathway to a breakthrough solution. Once this has been achieved it is then possible to construct the core of the solution. With this, and the associated work on converting the original UDEs into the desirable effects (DEs) the organisation wishes to see in place of the UDEs, the analysis is ready for the construction of the full solution. This ensures that stages two and three of the change process have been achieved – consensus on the direction of the solution and consensus on the benefits of the solution.

The final stage is to construct the implementation of the solution. This involves taking each element of the proposed solution, the feature set, and determining the obstacles that prevent implementation. It also involves examining each of the features and checking for any potential negative outcomes of implementing them. This whole activity uses two tools of the TOC/TP to arrive at consensus on overcoming all reservations to the proposed solution. There is only one stage left to complete – make it happen. It is at this point that many times people did not proceed. After spending all that time analysing and checking their problem set, the issues and conflicts it contains, developing the solution with clear logical analysis about how to achieve the objectives, nothing happened. For a fuller description of this process see Scheinkopf (1999) and Hutchin (2001).

At this point I started to use the TOC/TP tools to capture data about non-performance of implementation. This is where the research data collection process started.

The use of the undesirable effect (UDE) cloud

A specific use of the cloud technique is when analysing the type of conflicts which exist for people, when what they are trying to achieve is blocked in some way. This type of cloud is entitled an UDE cloud, first

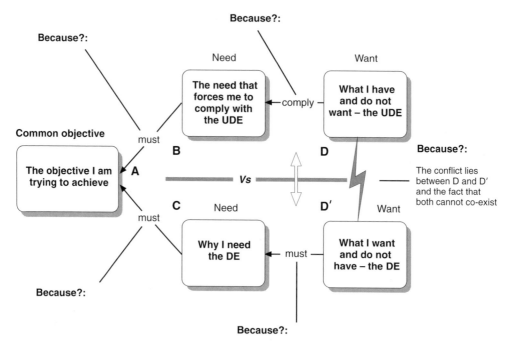

Fig. 5.1. The UDE cloud structure

described by Dr Goldratt at a conference in London in December 1993. The structure of the cloud remains the same as earlier, but the questions asked of each box are as shown in Fig. 5.1.

The raw materials for the cloud construction process are the UDEs that each person is experiencing within their area of operation. As noted earlier, this is where the real rigour enters the TOC process. It is vital that the UDEs are subjected to fierce scrutiny. They must withstand the harsh glare of analysis, are they negative? Is the statement a single entity? Does it have impact on the revenue chain of the organisation? Is it preventing improved performance with respect to the goal of the organisation? These questions must all be answered clearly and unequi-vocally.

Once the cloud has been constructed it can then be checked by first reading the cloud, then the surfacing of assumptions (Fig. 5.2). The level of rigour applied at this stage is vital if the cloud is to reveal the true nature of the conflict that exists. This starts with the nature of **D** and **D′**. In order to ensure clarity of conflict, the entries in the boxes must be a clear and precise statement of the entities. They should be writ-ten in present tense and be obviously in conflict. If the conflict is only apparent through the surfacing of assumptions between **D** and **D′** then the verbalisation requires further attention.

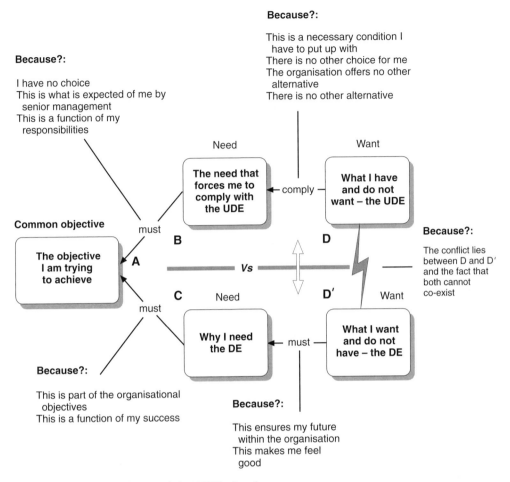

Fig. 5.2. The assumptions of the UDE cloud

Once all the boxes have been filled the strength of the cloud should be considered. This is checked by determining the impact of the cross-connection, that of **D** on **C** and that of **D'** on **B**. If **D** significantly, and negatively, impacts **C**, if **D** places **C** at risk, then that cross-connection is a powerful one. If the same applies to **D'** on **B** then the cloud is a particularly strong one. One such cross-connection is sufficient to give a cloud of some substance. Where both cross-connections are strong, then the cloud is extremely powerful.

The cross-connection (Fig. 5.3) demonstrates the power of the hold the UDE cloud possesses. Whatever is written in the **B** box is never in conflict with what is written in the **C** box. Indeed both are recognised as necessary conditions for the achievement of the goal, the objective which is written in the **A** box. This is what both the logic of the cloud structure and the

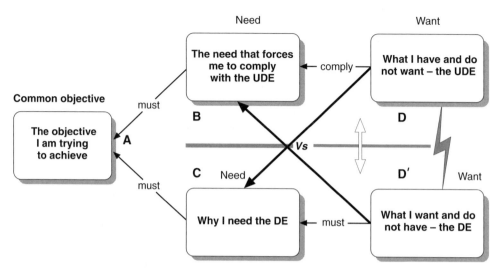

Fig. 5.3. *The cross-connection of the UDE cloud*

intuition of the individual speaks so vividly about. However, whatever is written in the **D** box clearly violates the existence of the **C** box and similarly what is written in the **D'** box clearly violates what is written in the **B** box. Thus the cloud is held in place. **D** is in conflict with **D'**, the present problem at odds with the desired future and there is no obvious way to remove **D**, which prevents **C** being achieved, while at the same time protecting **B** from the impact of **D'**.

There is one final check to determine the strength of the cloud. The nature of that written in the **B** box. The ability to check clouds comes with practice, the robustness of the UDEs, the power of the cross-connection, and the way in which the **B** box has been verbalised. One of the primary reasons why the UDE remains is also a function of the apparent conflict contained within the **B** box between the construct of the organisation and the construct of the individual. It is this unresolved conflict of constructs that ensures the continued existence of the UDE over the desirable effect, the DE. This is not easy to ascertain without practice. Whenever an UDE cloud is examined, often what is an assumption under the arrow from **A** to **B** or from **B** to **D** appears as the entry in the **B** box. The real content of the **B** box in an UDE cloud is always in itself a cloud. Each individual has a construct about their work, their relationships, their role and indeed themselves. Equally, through rules, procedures and measurements organisations' constructs also exist. It is the conflict between these two constructs that forms the entry to the **B** box in the UDE cloud.

These checks were used for all the clouds depicted within the case studies. There is a description of them with respect to project management in *Enterprise-focused management* (Hutchin 2001). For further descriptions of the cloud process see Cox and Spencer (1998), McMullen (1998) and Scheinkopf (1999).

Constructing the composite cloud

The process of building the composite cloud starts with collecting a reasonably large number of clouds from the data collected. These clouds were drawn from the available group of people, their companies and the range of problems they had chosen covered a substantial range of issues. It was not possible to select all the clouds collected. This was a decision made in line with the available time for the research and the restriction placed on me by other work. The only person involved in the analytical stage was myself. There were other people who could have been involved at this stage in terms of assisting with both collecting and initial analysis. However, the decision was taken not to include them at this point in order to keep the research process manageable. This was also in line with the decision not to try and explain the clouds in great detail, merely to capture them and from that to develop the generic cloud. I reasoned that this was an acceptable, and realistic, choice.

Once the group of clouds was chosen from the total set, the next step was to begin the process of building the composite cloud. This next step starts by examining the selected clouds chosen for a common thread. The process of selection starts with comparing two or three clouds at random to see if there is any pattern to the statements contained within the boxes. The first box chosen was the **D** box, then the **D'** and then on around the clouds in the sequence **C–A–B**. This sequence proved to be important as it was the **B** box which was to prove the most demanding when the generic cloud was being constructed and validated.

The ability to determine a pattern is rooted in the ability of the person doing the compilation. The first assumption that determined this approach was the skill and knowledge of the person carrying out the analysis. Without previous experience of both building and analysing clouds this would be a difficult activity. The second assumption is that it is a task best done by one person first and then the work of that person scrutinised by at least one other equally skilled practitioner. The third assumption is that such a person, in this case the researcher, has the skill to determine patterns from a wide range of initial conditions, problem areas and environments. Therefore it is unlikely that people without knowledge and experience of the problem areas, such as production or project management, would be able to determine the patterns that may or may not exist in clouds drawn from those problem areas.

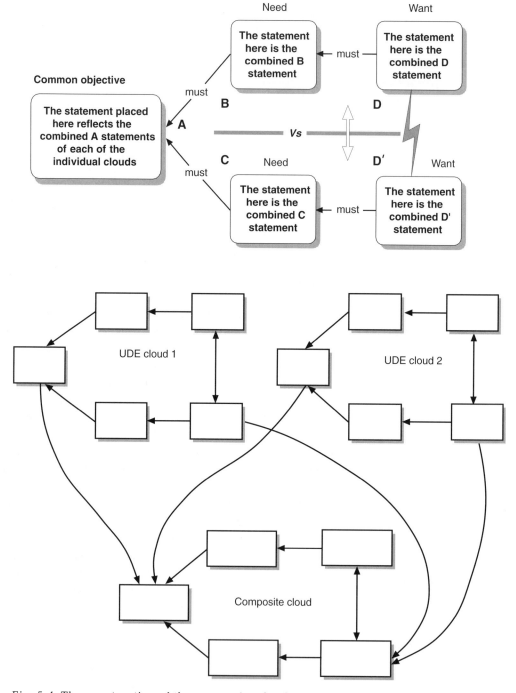

Fig. 5.4. The construction of the composite cloud

Therefore the construction of the composite cloud is accomplished by searching for a statement, which can be written in each box of the composite cloud, that encapsulates the equivalent entries in the individual UDE clouds. Fig. 5.4 shows this for the **A** and **D'** boxes, to complete the composite cloud this is continued until all the boxes have been filled.

Once the composite cloud is constructed it can then be used to check with specific examples to determine whether the composite cloud still applies. If this is the case then the composite cloud can be considered to be a generic cloud for the situation or situations being examined.

The remainder of this chapter outlines the case studies from which the clouds were collected and the environments in which they existed. In all 17 clouds are discussed drawn from the access given to myself. During the course of the research many more clouds were collected than described here. This selection, from 13 companies, four countries and over 350 people, is indicative of the range of issues described. In the next chapter the composite cloud is discussed which led to the creation of the generic cloud.

Introduction to the case studies

These case studies were developed over the period of involvement by myself of some five years in all. Each of the participating managers was involved in the creation of a solution to a particular problem within the organisation, and they were expected to implement the solution developed through the education/training which was taking place. What happened next was determined by the decision to proceed, or not. If the decision was to proceed then the process followed through to a logical conclusion and some degree of success was achieved. Throughout the whole of the research period this did occur, but does not form part of the study. This study focuses on those programmes where, at the same point as the successful implementation, the decision was taken not to proceed.

There were also occasions when the implementation stalled. In these cases this was due to an inadequate analysis at some point in the process, and the process itself pulled them back to correct the situation. In other words, there was a perfectly justifiable reason for not proceeding and the people themselves recognised this and stopped the implementation before any major additional problems occurred. Reasons included the take-over of the company with new management with new and different ideas about how to tackle the issues under review and changes in the market, which removed the pressure to deal with the problems being considered. Other reasons included the key people involved moving to new companies, or simply promoted to new roles elsewhere in the company.

The key feature for all of these reasons for not proceeding with the implementation is that they were clearly seen as valid and could be explained in a straightforward manner.

There were also situations where there were no such reasons for non-performance. This is where the issue of conflict arose. This could either be conflict with an individual or with a group. In other words, the non-performance and lack of successful implementation seemed dysfunctional, with no apparent reasons given. The case studies that follow are all examples of this last situation.

Case study 1

The division of this company that took part in the research is involved in supplying components to the automobile, industrial and civil engineering sectors throughout Europe and beyond. They are part of a multinational organisation but have their own corporate structure and facilities within the overall corporation, the headquarters of which are situated in the USA. They have about 1000 employees throughout Europe and their annual turnover is about £550 million. They use only a few basic raw materials and from that make a considerable range of products. Thus they can be thought of as a 'V' plant as described in Umble and Srikanth (1990). They have both manufacture and assembly operations, their own research and development resources and work directly with many of their customers, many of whom are very large organisations themselves. They have sites throughout Europe, and each site has manufacturing, customer support and sales resources.

The involvement with the company came about due to personal contact by the researcher to the manufacturing director for Europe who was keen to implement a process of on-going improvement throughout the company starting in the production area. At the time the company was experiencing difficulties in meeting customer demand for their products, their lead time was too long set against the industry standard and their competitors, and their due date performance was below 30%. The flow of material through the company was not coherent, with many blockages and constraints. They were experiencing an inability to schedule the four main plants in Europe to meet customer schedules. Other consultants had been brought in to address these issues but had so far produced no measurable improvement.

As part of the implementation of TOC some of the senior management team, ten in all, attended a three-day production workshop. They used this to ascertain the applicability of the TOC approach to their environment and the best way of proceeding if it was applicable. The outcome of this programme was the setting up of the main programme, which introduces the TOC known as the Jonah Programme, with ten people, including six of the first group and adding key people from their European operations and the Chief Executive Officer (CEO) for Europe. The tasks being addressed through the Jonah Programme included the ability to schedule across all plants in Europe, the development of a coherent quality policy throughout Europe, the development of a coherent information systems policy throughout the division, improving customer service. The full list is shown below with the subject matter they were responsible for as part of both their role within the company and the focus of their activities on the programme also identified.

- Bill (CEO): subject matter – how to improve the performance of the top team.
- David (manufacturing director): subject matter – how to develop and implement a European quality strategy.
- Helmut (German plant manager): subject matter – how to develop improved introduction of new products to manufacture.
- John (improvement manager): subject matter – how to improve the process of introducing improvement groups within manufacturing.
- Jean-Claude (European IT manager): subject matter – the introduction of a European inventory control system.
- Jonathon (European master scheduler): subject matter – the introduction of European scheduling linked to the inventory control system.

The remaining members of the team supported those already allocated a subject matter in line with the above list. The course proceeded as expected with each person completing a full analysis of his or her area of exploration and producing a solution to the problem. This was then prepared for implementation back in the company. Following this initial work a number of visits were undertaken by the researcher to check on progress and a number of production workshops were also held in order to lock the understanding and implementation of the TOC approach to production known as drum–buffer–rope to key people within the plants.

Throughout this time the CEO was trying to work on his subject matter and the issues it raised. Bill was in charge of the European Industrial Division with responsibility to improve the financial performance of the division, to ensure the highest possible customer satisfaction, to develop new markets particularly in the Far East and to improve the production facilities to meet 'world class' measures of performance. To achieve these goals he had recruited people from outside the company to bring in new ideas and techniques with the aim of encouraging the existing members of staff and to drive the company forward.

Bill found that the tasks and objectives set were not going to be easily achieved. During the Jonah Programme he recognised that some of the

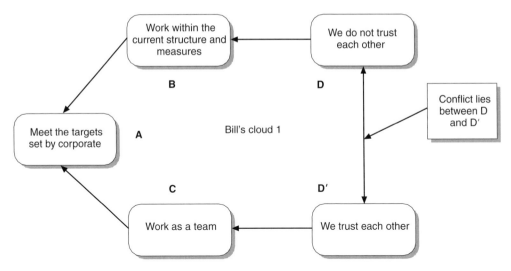

Fig. 5.5. The first cloud of the CEO

people who had been brought in were not up to the tasks set for them. Others seemed to have a different agenda from that set, and one appeared to have an agenda that did not include improving the performance of the business. Finally, others were not given the authority to do what they were supposed to do.

The first major complaint raised by Bill was that as a result of the debates that had been going on within the company, and the response to his repeated requests for action to be taken, there was a real lack of trust within the top team. They were each embarking on improvement plans for their areas without reference to each other, and often in conflict with each other. This led to the creation of the first cloud as outlined in Fig. 5.5.

The cloud was constructed based on the recognition by Bill that there was this lack of trust within his top team, between each of the members and also with himself and from him to the team. The objective of the cloud was clear to all members of the team, and agreed. From the perspective of Bill, a clear requirement was that the only way to achieve these goals was through the senior management group working as a team, and if they were to work as a team then they must trust each other. However, at the same time, the goals had to be accomplished through the existing structure and measure set by corporate and because of that there was a real lack of trust between the members of the senior management group, hence the conflict. The cloud was agreed by Bill as being a clear verbalisation of the conflict, the next step was to surface the assumptions. These are shown in Fig. 5.6.

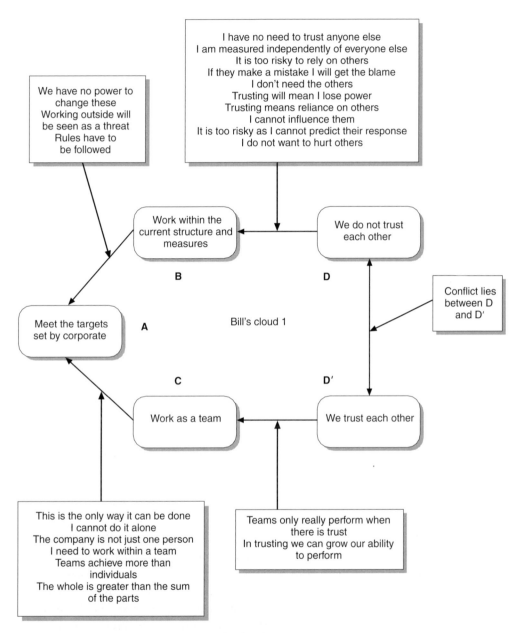

Fig. 5.6. Assumptions of the first CEO cloud

Examination of these assumptions revealed much about the way in which Bill wanted to run his division but at the same time revealed how the people who had been around the company for some time wanted to work, and this was due in no small way to the measures that were being used to determine performance and improvement. The surfacing of the

89

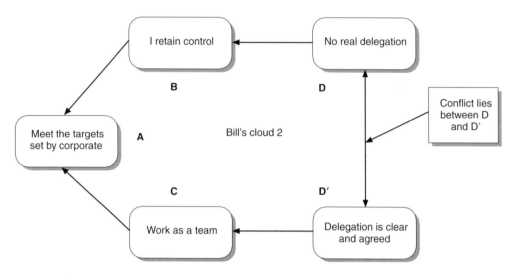

Fig. 5.7. Second CEO cloud

assumptions did suggest a number of possible options open to Bill but these were not taken. He felt that there was only one way to move forward. Therefore as a result of being unable to break this conflict the response of Bill was to assume ever-larger control over the day to day operation of the business in addition to the more strategic nature of his responsibilities. At the same time he took full responsibility for the development of the Far East operation which removed him from the day to day management of his division. This led to the creation of the second cloud outlined in Fig. 5.7.

Now the conflict was between the giving of clear delegation or not. The reading of the cloud from the objective to both **D** and **D'** was agreed as being clear and a fair description of the current situation. The main difference between this cloud and the first one was that in **B** he wrote, 'I retain control'. Again the next step was to surface assumptions (Fig. 5.8).

The assumptions surfaced here reflected the pain that Bill was now experiencing. In complying with the **D** in each of the two clouds so far, he knew he was compromising and that the compromise was hurting him greatly. The way in which he wanted to run the division was very much in line with the sequence from **A** through **C** to **D'**. For the moment, however, this approach lay in the future as there appeared to be no way in which to achieve what was required without going along the path from **A** through **B** to **D**, bearing in mind that **D** was a very undesirable effect to him personally.

What now became clear in this second cloud was the nature of what I came to describe as paradigm lock. The statement in **D'** is a desirable effect that the CEO wanted and believed in very much. He also knew that without this clear delegation he would not be able to develop the

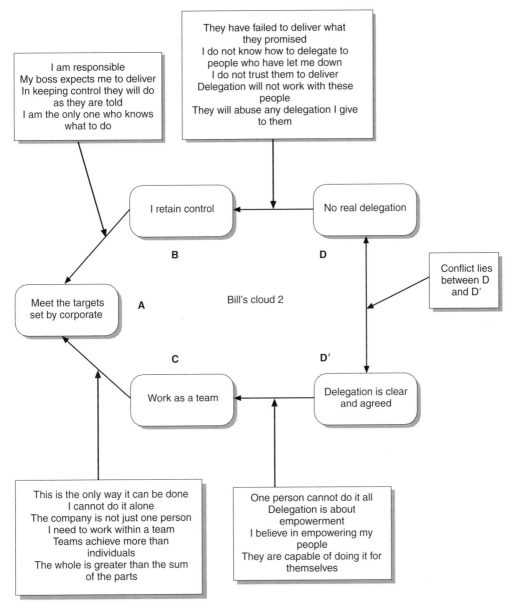

Fig. 5.8. Second cloud assumptions

team method of working he felt was necessary to achieve the goals set by corporate. However, to move to that state would be to put in jeopardy the other requirement in **B**. Because there was no apparent way to achieve **D'** without risking **B** the only avenue open was to continue with the undesirable effect in **D** and accept the risks involved. This method of working with top teams was alien to the CEO but he felt he had no

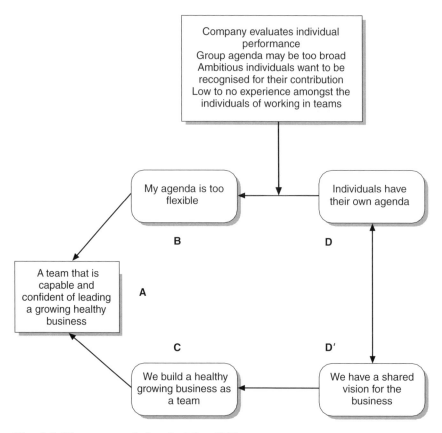

Fig. 5.9. The personal cloud of the CEO

other choice. Even though the assumptions were examined and some were recognised as erroneous no action was taken. The reason being given was that the risk to **B** was too great to consider any other option at all. Recognising this state of affairs he then took time to construct an additional cloud in which he tried to verbalise his feelings towards the team in greater detail. This cloud is shown in Fig. 5.9.

This cloud allowed him to develop just what he was looking for in the top team. He considered that the objective as stated was important to him because he felt that a team is a more powerful and effective way of running a business rather than through a single individual, that more complex challenges can be addressed by a well functioning top team, that a team would allow the company to have a greater diversity of background and contributions than a hierarchical organisation, and finally that this environment would create a self-sustaining model that competitors would not be able to break. He was then asked to surface the assumptions under the arrows. Those that sat beneath **A–C** were that he felt that he could build a team in Europe even though the culture was not supportive, that his team wanted to work this way and there was a healthy growing business available to them with the existing set of competencies. The assumptions that sat under the arrow from **A** to **B** were that people are self-regulating, that his people wanted to work in the teams, that the priorities and the group agenda were clear and agreed.

He was then asked to consider why **D**$'$ was so important to him and gave the following reasons

- that a shared vision creates a powerful force for success
- a shared vision creates commitment
- a shared vision enables quicker resolution of conflicts in priorities
- creating vision will build top teams
- our business will not grow without shared vision
- a shared vision helps define collective responsibility
- a shared vision requires individual/personal assessment of fit with the company.

This led to a consideration of what needs made **D**$'$ so important and these were listed as below

- an aligned, committed team is the only way to create and sustain a growing healthy business
- the business at the time was not growing
- he doubted the future with the current technology base within the company
- people want to be part of a successful business
- people will feel more comfortable by being part of a successful team
- people are mature enough to work in a team
- we can create our own successful culture by building the business as a team
- we have the capability among the top team to create a healthy growing business.

Once these had been identified the next stage was to consider why the cloud was in existence, in other words the assumptions that lay beneath **B–D** and why he allowed **D** to continue in existence. The reasons for **D** are shown in the Fig. 5.9. The reasons for the continued existence of the **B–D** arrow were given as

- people will see the big (group) picture and take initiative to align their agenda with the group agenda
- people will accept collective responsibility for the business
- people will work together to resolve cross-functional issues without his continued intervention
- people want to resolve their own problems

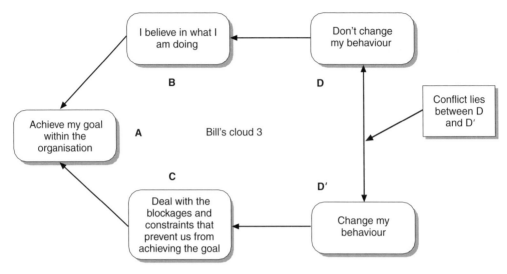

Fig. 5.10. The third CEO cloud

- he is willing to compromise his agenda if he sees a clear need from one of the staff members to spend time on theirs
- he can make up the time lost on his agenda after hours
- he assumes their judgement is sound and that they are comfortable exercising it
- he shares with his people the same basic assumptions
- flexibility creates room for taking new opportunities
- he has to allow time for frequent priority changes from corporate
- there are too many priorities.

Once these clouds had been developed and considered it was then possible to construct a cloud that might be more generic in application (Fig. 5.10). Here the verbalisation has been changed to show the generic nature of the conflicts faced by the CEO and the following case studies will try to examine whether this is such a generic cloud or not. If so then the cloud should be capable of application beyond this research.

The objective of the cloud is now verbalised as 'achieve my goal within the organisation'. For the CEO the goal in question was still the original objective. The cloud can now be read as

> *In order to achieve that objective it is necessary to deal with the blockages and constraints that prevent such achievement, and in order to do that I must change my behaviour. On the other hand, in order to achieve my goal within the organisation I must believe in what I am doing, and in order to do that I must not change my behaviour.*

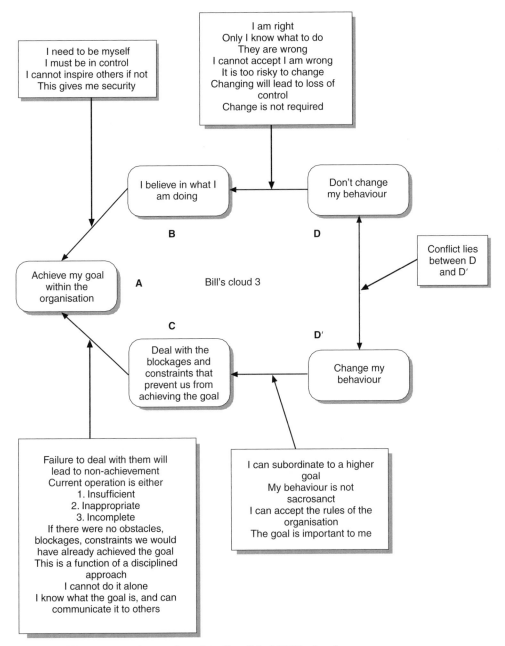

Fig. 5.11. The assumptions related to the third CEO cloud

The next step was the surfacing of the assumptions that lie behind the arrows and these are shown in Fig. 5.11.

This cloud, and the assumptions that were surfaced, was clearly defined as blocking the CEO from taking any action. The reason being that in

95

order to move to D', any injection that would achieve that desirable effect would put in jeopardy the entity **B**. This was seen as too threatening. The inability to see that both **B** and **C** could combine in any way was sufficient to block any progress towards the achievement of D'. There was no way in which **B** and **C** could co-exist; there was no perceived overlap of these two entities, and no process that could achieve such an overlap. Although **B** and **C** were not in conflict, the CEO saw no way to achieve both, and even if they could exist together, he saw no process capable of achieving such an impossible task. The implications for **B** should D' be accomplished were too great a risk to consider. The change itself was too threatening for **B** and therefore **B** became the goal of the CEO rather than that set by corporate, or even by the group.

As a result of this inaction the CEO took actions, which led to others leaving the company, including some whose purpose had been to implement exactly what the CEO wanted. This action led to the inability of the CEO to meet the targets set out by corporate in the USA. This in turn brought about a change at the top of the organisation where the CEO was removed from his position and given the task of marketing new products to the Far East and a new CEO being appointed. Although the original CEO did not leave the company he now had a greatly reduced role within the company and greatly reduced power. This continued for a further twelve months and Bill has now left the company and is working as a consultant in the USA. Of the other members of the team that took part in the programme some are still in the company, others have left and in three cases have come back to me for further work in their new organisations. The reason given for coming back was that they thought, indeed knew, that the TOC/TP could deliver, but not with the CEO they had in the previous company. Now that constraint had gone they felt able to put their new companies on a process of on-going improvement using the TOC/TP.

Case study 2

The second case study comes from a company involved in the manufacture of automotive parts. The story centres on the manufacturing director and his attempts to put the company on a process of on-going improvement. Peter was brought in by the CEO to sort out the problems related to production throughout the division, to recruit where appropriate and to implement the latest manufacturing approaches including cell manufacture, Kanban and drum–buffer–rope. Many of the problems they faced were similar to those of the first case study.

Peter started with the production workshop with some of his people and then moved to the Jonah Programme. As the programmes progressed the

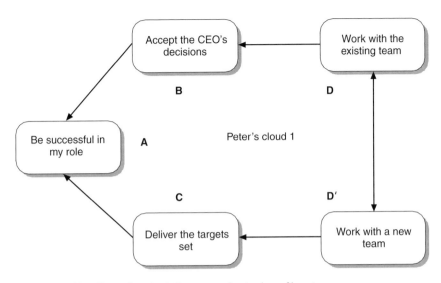

Fig. 5.12. The first cloud of the manufacturing director

level of frustration and anger felt by Peter grew. This anger and frustration centred on the structure that the CEO had set up and the impact this had on the whole production area. Although the CEO had given Peter the authority to recruit people, which he did, he also found that he was not able to influence appointments, which, although they were not strictly in the production area, had considerable impact nevertheless. One example of this was in the area of purchasing. At the same time the CEO made it clear that no changes to the top team were envisaged and that they would

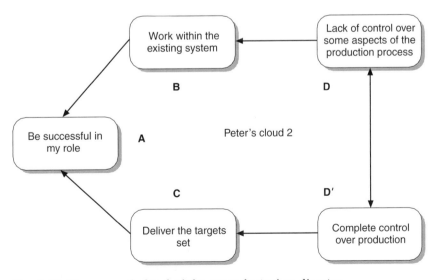

Fig. 5.13. The second cloud of the manufacturing director

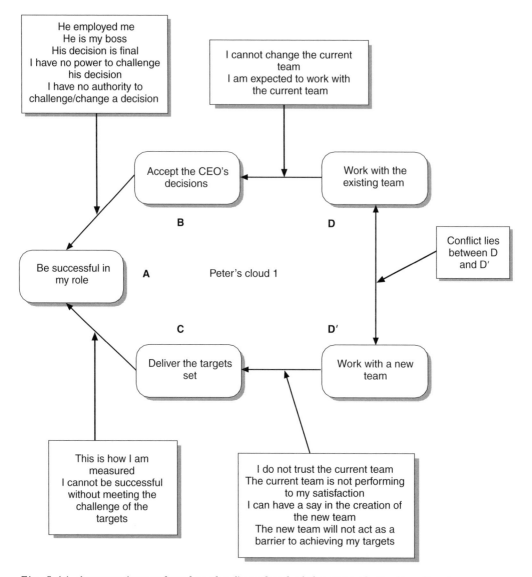

He employed me
He is my boss
His decision is final
I have no power to challenge his decision
I have no authority to challenge/change a decision

I cannot change the current team
I am expected to work with the current team

Accept the CEO's decisions

Work with the existing team

B

D

Conflict lies between **D** and **D'**

Be successful in my role

A

Peter's cloud 1

C

D'

Deliver the targets set

Work with a new team

This is how I am measured
I cannot be successful without meeting the challenge of the targets

I do not trust the current team
The current team is not performing to my satisfaction
I can have a say in the creation of the new team
The new team will not act as a barrier to achieving my targets

Fig. 5.14. Assumptions related to the first cloud of the manufacturing director

have to work together. This led to the development of the first cloud as shown in Fig. 5.12.

This was very much a conflict between what he wanted now and what he wanted to change to. His original intention was to change the team with the support of the CEO in order to alleviate the other cloud, which was affecting him. This is shown in Fig. 5.13.

Once this cloud had been verbalised in discussion, he changed his original **D** to the one in Fig. 5.13, namely 'lack of control over some aspects

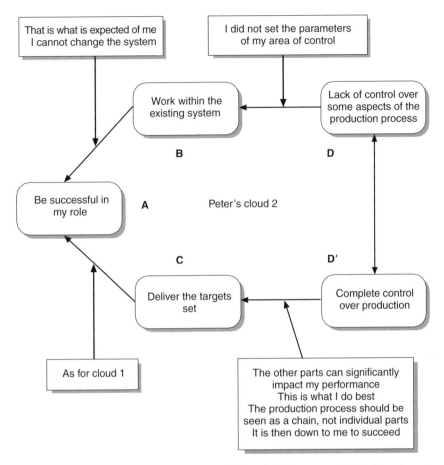

Fig. 5.15. Assumptions related to the second cloud of the manufacturing director

of the production process'. His main problem was that although he was responsible for production, he was not responsible for purchasing or distribution, both of which were controlled by another director. These two clouds were therefore linked through the team he had to work with and the ability to achieve the targets set by both the CEO and the market. Once the clouds had been verbalised, the next step was to surface the assumptions (Fig. 5.14).

This cloud was the first time in which the impact of **D**′ on the continued existence of **B** was recognised. If a new team was to be formed within the company, then there was the possibility of a real challenge to the CEO's decisions, which, given the nature of the CEO's own clouds, was unlikely to happen. At the same time the second cloud was also examined through the surfacing of assumptions and is shown in Fig. 5.15.

The two clouds combined to give Peter a clear view of the predicament he was in. To his mind the lack of control over the whole of the production

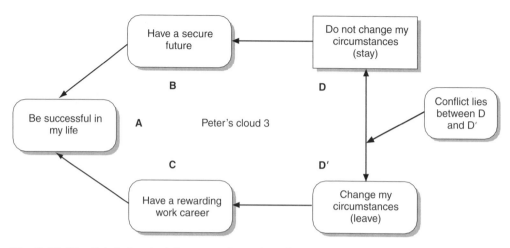

Fig. 5.16. The third cloud of the manufacturing director

process was a major factor in his inability to meet the targets set by the CEO. The other director, he felt, was playing a political game in which he did not want to participate. This struggle continued for some eight months during which time he decided that either the CEO would change the structure and the span of control or he would have to leave. This then led to the creation of the final cloud which is shown in Fig. 5.16.

This cloud was developed in my office while considering what Peter should do. The assumptions were surfaced and centred on the need of the person to feel at home with what he was doing in his life, and even though leaving was a possible threat to his **B**, staying meant that both **A** and **C** could never be achieved. Although there was a potential threat from **D'** to **B** the bigger threat was from the continued existence of **D** and the threat that contained for **C**.

Within five months of verbalising this cloud the CEO and Peter argued over policy concerning production and the top team and Peter resigned with immediate effect. Within two weeks he had set himself up as an independent manufacturing consultant, drawing on his experience prior to joining this company, and was also successful in gaining a position within a larger manufacturing consultancy, the combination of both giving him the security he needed. He continues to work in this position and uses the TOC/TP where he feels it is most appropriate.

Case study 3

This case study involves a company which was involved in the research and design, manufacture and on-going support of telecommunication equipment. The company was formed in two distinct divisions, each being a separate business unit. The first focused on the terminal equipment and the second on the base stations, which are sited throughout the country. They have about 500 employees in the UK and their turnover is in the region of £100 million. They are a high technology company using the latest technological developments in both communications and microprocessors to maintain a leading competitive edge in a difficult market with a high potential for increasing revenues to the company, which can keep ahead of the competition, or to develop a new dimension to the product. A great deal of resources is therefore given to the engineering function, which includes research and development of new products. There is also a great deal of pressure to bring products to market as quickly as possible. This in turn places a great deal of pressure on both engineering and marketing. The company was then owned jointly, by two major companies in the field of telecommunications, with no other shareholders.

The manufacturing environment is relatively simple, with the part of the business that manufactures the telephones, known as terminals, being a simple line with assembly operations throughout the whole procedure. This equates to the description of an 'A' plant while the base stations area, called infrastructure, is different in that it conforms to the description of a 'T' plant. Both of these types are fully described in Umble and Srikanth (1990). Both of these manufacturing areas are managed separately, and submit accounts and all other management information as two separate organisations under the same umbrella.

The approach to myself came after the business development manager attended a seminar run by Dr Goldratt and a follow-up meeting with the researcher. This led to the commencement of a detailed and comprehensive programme, which included production workshops and the Jonah Programme. They were experiencing a number of problems such as delays in getting new products to market, being unable to meet customer due dates, ever growing lead times for manufacturing, and this in both areas. The programmes were spread over a twelve month period and involved some 50 people, with ten attending the Jonah Programme. The production workshops were designed to introduce the drum–buffer–rope solution to both manufacturing areas.

The Jonah Programme included people from both of the business units and was drawn from manufacturing, engineering, sales and marketing, and business development. The key areas to address were agreed upon prior to the commencement and included the time taken to bring new products to market, the delays in manufacturing which were leading to missed due dates and quite severe problems within the manufacturing area and, in particular, the question of problems related to suppliers. As part of the programmes adopted by the company the two prime movers were the business development manager, Sean, and the sales and marketing manager, Mike. These two people were responsible for attacking the current problems within the company and for selecting the people they thought would best be able to deliver the necessary solutions. Sean had followed the managing director (MD) from a previous company where they had worked together successfully. The MD relied on Sean to identify areas of concern and come up with solutions to address these problems, often including their implementation. For the Jonah Programme, each person attending was asked to consider the area under their control and responsibility, and to then determine what they wanted to address through the programme.

The response of the group is shown below.

Team 1   Andy (engineering manager): subject matter – to implement a process of continuous concept to product lead-time improvement.

The efficient process of meeting market demand needs cost effective implementation in the form of manufacturable products, which will directly impact the company's competitive ability in the market. This will lead to a larger product portfolio, a reduction in cycle times, a reduction in costs and an increase in the company profits. The current problems associated with this are

(1) product developments are late
(2) development costs are over budget
(3) full-scale developments are slow in starting
(4) some market needs are not satisfied by our products
(5) unit costs are high
(6) manufacture starts slowly
(7) there are insufficient development funds to meet the business objectives
(8) some staff morale is low
(9) some senior managers are not trusted.

Team 1   Bob (production manager): subject matter – to reduce the manufacturing cycle time of the production process. The problems is this area being

(1)   there is a shortage of some parts
(2)   we are failing to deliver some customer orders on time
(3)   there is too much rework
(4)   some test equipment is unreliable
(5)   some supplied parts do not meet the spec
(6)   the shop floor data collection system does not locate the products
(7)   parts not arriving from stores when required

(8)   the cost of rework is not known

(9)   RF board has to double back to fit gasket after test

(10) the telephone top cover has to be cut by hand

(11) the heatbonding machine is not reliable

(12) production layout does not complement the product flow.

Team 2   Chris (marketing manager): subject matter – to improve the turn-around time for the preparation of quotations to customers typically from around five days to two days (working days). Typical problems being

(1)   some people delay their decision on approving the pricing: Approval (PA)

(2)   pricing data takes too long to obtain

(3)   people look for reasons to reject PAs

(4)   it is difficult to get agreement on prices

(5)   it is difficult to get agreement on timescales

(6)   too many people are required as signatories

(7)   engineering cannot guarantee costs

(8)   there are inaccurate requirements

(9)   there are customer misunderstandings

(10) there are unrealistic internal timescales

(11) there is a long waiting time for quotations from subcontractors

(12) there are manipulative politics

(13) some people fail to deliver what they promised.

Team 2   Frank (engineering manager): subject matter – to improve the quality and speed of design into manufacture by introducing more process engineering into core product design, and the introduction of structured methods of product introduction e.g. increased design involvement in factory test equipment development/auditing.

   Benefits include a reduction in development time and costs, the avoid-ance of costly mistakes by analysis of core product introduction in advance of development, the reduction in overlap of effort/repeat of effort and thus a reduction in firefighting, allowing for more products to be developed, and allowing for better control of suppliers by a clearer understanding of the roles of engineering design, production engineering and materials management. The key problems were identified as

(1)   development costs are over budget

(2)   some unit costs are over budget

(3)   there are additional processes in manufacturing not known at this early stage

(4)   there is late detection of manufacturing problems

(5)   there is a lack of initiative in solving problems

(6) there is rework

(7) there is duplication of effort

(8) there is protracted production handover

(9) there are unplanned corrective actions

(10) some products are difficult to rework

(11) some components get damaged during assembly

(12) some planning is inaccurate

(13) some suppliers do not meet our requirements

(14) some products are difficult to manufacture.

Team 1   John (senior production manager): subject matter – to improve the process of design into manufacture by improving planning, reducing timescales, reducing re-engineering and increasing the ability to meet production ramp up demand within the business unit. The problems identified were

(1) there is a failure to achieve design performance

(2) products are difficult to manufacture

(3) there is often rework of manufacturing systems

(4) manufacturing engineering time is lost

(5) there are product design changes

(6) changes take too long

(7) communication is difficult between design and manufacture

(8) there is a mismatch between milestones and key dates

(9) sometime performance deviates from the plan.

Team 2   Mark (production manager): subject matter – to give our customers confidence in our delivery promises so they will place further orders. This is to be achieved by identifying the constraints, which restrict our performance, and taking action to diminish or remove them. The initial problems being

(1)   customer's delivery dates are sometimes missed

(2)   manufacture sometimes fails to meet production targets

(3)   production constraints are not fully understood

(4)   some of the production process times are inaccurate

(5)   there are material shortages

(6)   some suppliers do not meet our requirements

(7)   stock records are not accurate

(8)   the release of Bills of Materials (BOMs) for new products is often late

(9)   some sales forecasts are often inaccurate

(10) there is rework

(11) the production layout does not complement production flow

(12) the parts are not arriving from stores when required.

Team 1/2 Mike (senior sales manager): subject matter – to make the business unit marketing function operate more effectively. The effectiveness of my group will have a direct impact on the profitability of the terminals business. The objectives are to exceed the business unit contribution in 1994/95 by 10% while reducing the marketing budget by 20%. The problems centred on the list below

(1) company is not perceived as a good supplier by customers
(2) company has no consumer image
(3) sales are low
(4) engineering do not support the new product plan
(5) margins are continually being eroded
(6) confidence in shipment dates is low
(7) the distribution base is low
(8) the department is always firefighting
(9) distributors do not have confidence in our product reliability
(10) new products and accessories are always late to the market.

Team 2 Neil (senior production manager): subject matter – to consistently improve the overall performance of the production facility and to increase the volume through the plant by at least 20%. The main problems were considered to be

(1) there is limited capital budget to invest in all production processes
(2) there is scrap
(3) there are rejects
(4) there are customer complaints
(5) there are returns from customers
(6) there is a lack of resource flexibility
(7) the capital depreciation is high.

Team 2 Richard (sales and marketing support manager): subject matter – to reduce timescales for projects from concept to production and at the same time improve the product introduction to the factory. The problems identified in this area were

(1) agreed project milestones are not met
(2) project requirements are not clear
(3) unplanned customer changes occur
(4) there is a lack of some resources
(5) unforeseen technical problems occur
(6) we are always firefighting
(7) some people lack motivation
(8) there is a mismatch of skills to the workload

(9) there is protracted production handover
(10) some managers are not prepared to commit themselves
(11) there is poor communication with marketing.

Team 1/2 Sean (business development manager): subject matter – the objective is to examine how to function as a catalyst in order to initiate and co-ordinate improvements to the business process. The problems that lie in this area are

(1) some people are resistant to changes which affect them
(2) some people feel too busy to take on change
(3) some people believe that they do not need to improve
(4) some people believe everybody else needs to improve
(5) some people will agree to improvements but do not implement them
(6) some people are unable to overcome historic conflicts
(7) there is a lack of necessary skills
(8) there is insufficient imagination
(9) some links in the business process are not being improved
(10) there is inaccurate measurement of the contribution of improvement initiatives
(11) some suppliers do not match our requirements.

The programmes were completed with the normal outcome of each person working with their own implementation plan for the resolution of the problem they started with. Each team followed up the Jonah Programme with four production workshops for a total of 32 people from the production area with the aim of securing the implementation of drum–buffer–rope. As a result of this both teams knew what had to be done in the implementation plan.

In one half of the company, team 2, these solutions were implemented fully. They were able to obtain the improvements they were seeking. The volume went up from 600 units in a 20-day lead-time to 2500 units in 4 days. The due date performance was held at 100% for most of that time, only slipping below when suppliers were late or some other unforeseen problem occurred. Neil, the senior production manager, left at the start of this process and was replaced by Mark who had been his understudy. Neil continues to keep in touch although he has had no other opportunity to apply TOC/TP to any of his subsequent companies. The base station side of the business has grown from strength to strength. Richard has taken over as the division chief and Mark has taken on the role of quality manager in addition to his production duties.

However in the other half, team 1, where Mike and Sean were most involved very little happened. Although the plans were sound, they were given little opportunity to come to fruition as the MD made a decision to change the senior management structure. This involved moving Sean to become head of engineering and forcing Mike to take actions in which he did not believe. This shift was driven by the lack of results coming from team 1 and the fact that Andy and Frank left shortly after completion of the Jonah Programme. The remaining team members felt they did not have the necessary skills to continue and so stopped altogether.

With these changes, over the next few months both Mike and Sean grew in frustration as the plans that had been so carefully developed were put completely to one side, a new director was brought in by the MD over the heads of both men and this new person wanted to do things his own way without reference to any work that had gone on before. After six months this was recognised by the MD as having been a mistake and he then lay the blame for this at the feet of both Sean and Mike. It was at this point that both clouds were developed as the two men entered a phase of combined frustration and depression.

The first cloud is that of Sean and the second, that of Mike (Figs. 5.17 to 5.19). The conflict in both cases was the same, staying against leaving. The need that staying was required for was different for both men, equally the need that leaving was trying to support was also different, but in debate both could agree that the **B** for one was equally appropriate to the other and the same for **C** and indeed for **A**. Once the initial clouds had been verbalised the next step was to surface the assumptions that led to the creation of the cloud in the first place. It is also important to

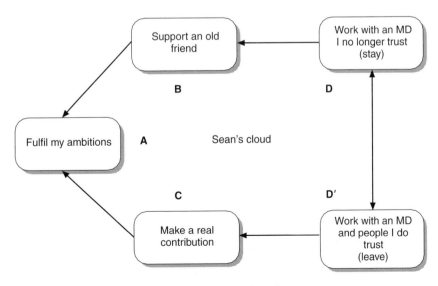

Fig. 5.17. The first cloud of the business development manager

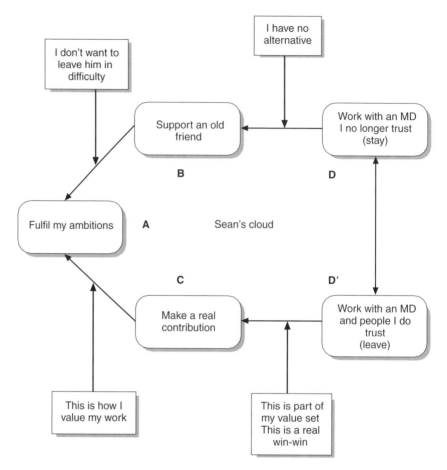

Fig. 5.18. Assumptions related to the first cloud of the business development manager

recognise that the conflict was verbalised as internal to each of them, the MD although a player was not the key figure. It was their own personal conflict that was deemed to be of greatest importance.

Although the first verbalisation was about the conflict related to trust in first the MD and then others within the company the real conflict that emerged was between staying or leaving, and this became the same for both of them. Being able to verbalise the cloud to this level of detail was not an easy task as it required each of them to look inside themselves and ask questions of themselves which they admitted afterwards they did not like to do, although they also accepted that without such inward examination any resulting analysis would have been of little value. At this point, using the interaction of **D**′ on the existence of **B**, in both cases **D**′ was seen as a threat to the continued existence of **B**.

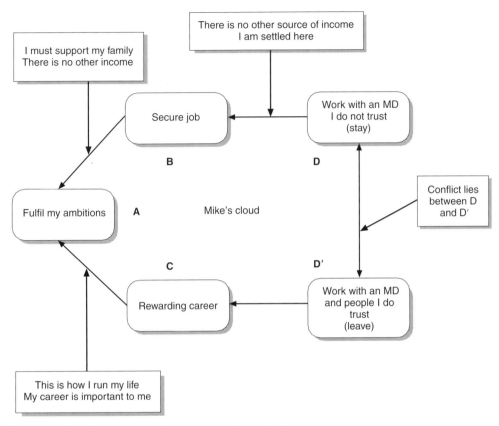

Fig. 5.19. The first cloud of the sales and marketing manager

In the case of the business development manager the friendship with the MD went back some time and was not easy to give up, even though staying involved an increasing amount of personal pain. The only reason he had agreed to switch to the head of engineering was to comply with a request from the MD; he being of the opinion that he was not qualified to be head of engineering. The fact that he was subsequently successful in the post for some twelve months and in that time brought a major new product to the market was not seen as particularly relevant, simply engineering was not where he saw his career going.

The surfacing of the assumptions only served to reinforce the nature of the conflict and give added impetus to the need to break it. It soon became obvious that Sean would have to seriously consider where he was going in his career and that it would inevitably mean a break with the past. Sean eventually left and joined a new company, first as head of engineering and, more recently, as director of manufacture. He is still using TOC/TP and is currently waiting to put this new company on the relevant TOC/TP programmes.

The cloud developed by Mike (Fig. 5.19) was similar although there was no previous working relationship with the MD.

Again with this cloud, once it had been verbalised the cross impact of **D**$'$ on **B** was examined. Mike saw leaving the company as a major threat to his family, they being young and relying totally on him for income. The outcome was that he telephoned the researcher after about six months informing him that he was leaving the company with no job to go to and could they meet. The meeting took place close to where Mike lives and confirmed that the reasons for leaving were the conditions that now existed within that division and that they were now intolerable as far as Mike was concerned. He is now with a new company and enjoying life again, and using TOC/TP within that new organisation.

An overview of three further case studies

These remaining case studies are in all cases similar to those already described. What are covered in these studies are the clouds that were developed during or just after the programmes with respect to the management of the programmes and the implementations, and the relationships between the people in the organisations. Although not developed to the same degree as the preceding three case studies, the circumstances are the same. Each company was involved in the implementation of the TOC/TP and the individuals concerned had come up against a conflict of the same type as before.

Case study 4

This next example is drawn from a Jonah Programme in 1993. The company was a small manufacturing company. Jim was the owner of the company and he brought his top team to the programme with the aim of ensuring that they were able to run the business after he retired. His first concern was about whether the TOC/TP was of value to him and his company, which led to the creation of the first cloud shown in Fig. 5.20.

Jim invested in the TOC/TP through two Jonah Programmes and three production workshops. In all some 20 people attended TOC/TP programmes. The operations director was given the task of implementing the drum–buffer–rope. However, the timescale started to slip, as it became obvious that the way in which the improvements were being handled was creating problems between the members of the top team. Jim started to feel that his investment in the people at the top was not being returned in the form of better performance. He was also keen to sell as soon as he could and was afraid that any delay would lead to a

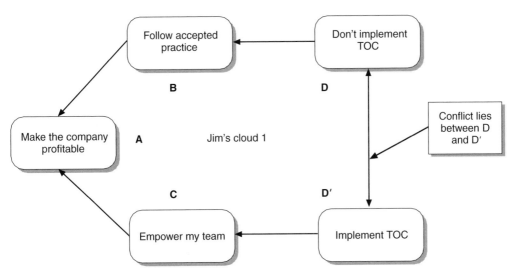

Fig. 5.20. The first cloud of the chairman

reduction in the price the company would attract. Hence the second cloud was constructed (Fig. 5.21).

As time went by and the performance only improved in short bursts, Jim began to push the team hard. They were continually fighting over strategy in the market, the sales and marketing team were pushing ahead with new product launches, but production could not keep up. This was even after significant improvement in lead-time and capacity through the drum–buffer–rope implementation. Every time that production was able

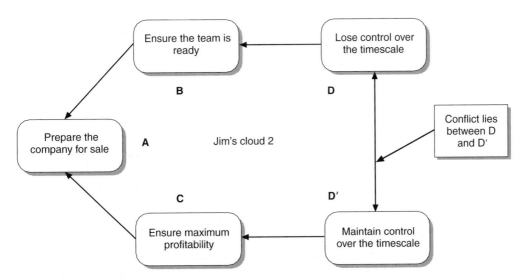

Fig. 5.21. The second cloud of the chairman

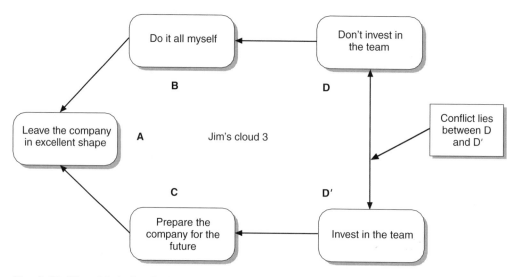

Fig. 5.22. The third cloud of the chairman

to create some spare capacity, which in turn gave protection to the plant and to the customers, the sales people would sell that capacity and therefore remove the protection. This in turn meant that production was never able to really get to grips with their problems. This is not a new phenomenon and had been pointed out to them by the researcher, but they ignored the advice and continued to try and sell more every time capacity became available. As this continued the level of fighting between the top team grew ever more difficult to control. The result was that Jim finally took more and more control and in the end sold the company without much reference to the rest of the team. His patience had given out. The cloud is shown in Fig. 5.22.

Jim felt that **D'** was no longer a viable option and took the risk that not investing in the team might have a negative impact on the sale of the company. In the end he left the company having sold it for a reasonable price. Of the top team only two remain. The operations director left shortly after and is now running a new company using TOC/TP in both production and sales.

At the time the operations director was taking a lot of criticism for the performance of his area. At every meeting with the top team, however, he always took the blame on himself, never his people. In discussions with the researcher he produced the cloud in Fig. 5.23.

He felt that the only way to produce the results that he and Jim wanted was to push his people gently, encouraging them to grow in knowledge and contribution. In the end, however, the non-performance of his people led to his leaving the company.

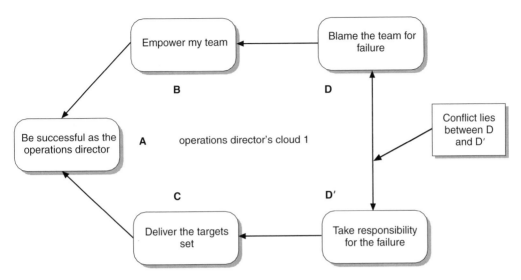

Fig. 5.23. The first cloud of the operations director

Case study 5

The next company was based in Germany and was involved in making household and bathroom fittings and furniture. They attended four programmes, the management skills workshop (MSW) and three production workshops. The total number of people attending programmes being eleven on the MSW and senior management production workshops and 20 people attending the five day production workshops.

Their primary aim was to introduce drum–buffer–rope into the company and then to move to the Jonah Programme in order to develop new markets and new sales opportunities. They were successful in reducing the leadtime of their manufacturing process and were starting to achieve much better due date performance when a particular problem arose. The owner of the company had expected to have a considerable amount of money paid to him at the end of the financial year. However, due to the market downturn this was not possible. Also, as a result of our activities with drum–buffer–rope, excess capacity had been revealed. The owner took this opportunity to convert the spare capacity into money by making 35 people redundant. These people were from the areas that had improved and from which it was hoped more sales could be generated. With this action the owner lost the opportunity to develop the markets he was already in and any chance of developing new ones. At this point the researcher pulled out of the company. The MD of the company, Hans, constructed the cloud shown in Fig. 5.24.

The decision to make so many people redundant was not something that Hans wanted to contemplate. For him it was against all that he

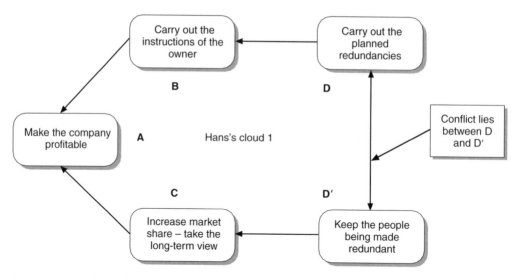

Fig. 5.24. The first cloud of the managing director

believed in when it comes to running a successful manufacturing company. However, the second cloud (Fig. 5.25) was also applicable and made life very difficult.

The result was that Hans waited for a few weeks and then left the company. At the same time the technical director also left the company feeling that the owner had destroyed his work and did not run the plant the way it should be. The technical director was a Jonah from a previous company the researcher had been involved with. Both are still in touch with the

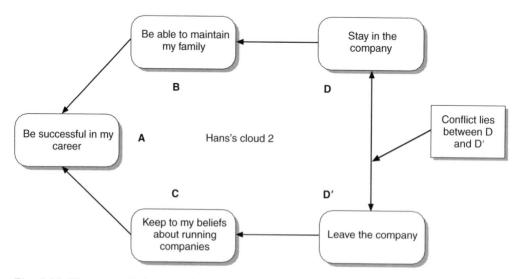

Fig. 5.25. The second cloud of the managing director

researcher and are keen to develop more understanding of the TOC/TP and the way it applies to their companies.

Case study 6

The final company to be examined was a small consultancy practice. It was using TOC/TP as the basis for its operations. The researcher came to work with it as he was developing his own understanding of TOC/TP. Stacey was one of the original members of the group, which had come together in 1991. She had been exposed to the work of Dr Goldratt in 1987 and continued to develop understanding throughout that period. The first cloud (Fig. 5.26) refers to the way in which she felt about working with some of the people in the practice. This was a real issue for her as the code of practice was clear but at the same time she could not come to terms with the non-performance of other members of the team.

This led to a real breakdown in communication between Stacey and the rest of the team. Once more the cross-connection of the cloud, the impact of **D'** on **B** and that of **D** on **C** was fierce. Stacey felt trapped.

This level of feeling trapped was not helped when the head of the practice made it clear that the finger-pointing and the blame culture that had developed was not to be tolerated and that he expected them to sort it out using the TOC/TP tools. At this point the second cloud (Fig. 5.27) became very real to Stacey.

Stacey found that she had to ask very searching questions of herself and where she was going in her life. This was not a comfortable period for her

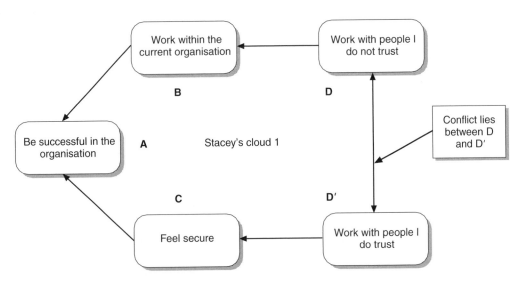

Fig. 5.26. The first cloud of the consultant

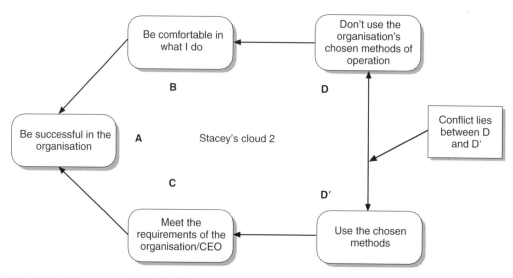

Fig. 5.27. *The second cloud of the consultant*

and the pain of staying in the organisation was matched by the thought of leaving. At the time of writing Stacey is still in the organisation but is very much a peripheral figure with no real input on both day to day operations and long-term strategy.

Review of chapter 5

This chapter has been concerned with an examination of the data collected as part of this research. In most cases the clouds were developed at the time. Some were developed over time during which the individual was able to verbalise better the issues faced. It was observed that when the impact of a cloud was felt the level of emotion was high. Each of the clouds presented as part of the case studies were only a small fraction of the total number encountered during the time of the study. The conflicts depicted within each cloud are always a function of strong emotion on the part of the owner of the cloud. The time taken to verbalise each cloud is both a function of this emotion and the skill of the researcher in developing them. The latter improved over the time of the research considerably. At the same time the ability to surface the assumptions also grew in both competence and confidence. As a result of this, it is now relatively straightforward to teach the cloud process in this way and for the individual to resolve these types of conflict without recourse to any outside party.

The point of breakdown in the implementation process was found to be the point at which unresolvable conflict appeared. The clouds represent the level and types of conflict which prevented the successful completion of the improvement project. The TOC/TP approach had been instrumental in bringing the individual to the point of recognition that there was a conflict and that the success or otherwise of the improvement now depended on the removal of that conflict.

CHAPTER SIX

Analysing the data

This chapter is concerned with a deeper analysis of the case studies described in chapter 5. It begins with the creation of a composite cloud derived from those discussed in the previous chapter. This is followed by a discussion of the iteration that took place and a composite cloud is presented which, it is argued, is a generic cloud acting as an obstacle to the implementation of change. The chapter then returns to the change models first presented in chapter 2 and revises them in the light of this generic cloud. Finally, a theory is presented for one aspect of non-performance in implementing change and this is linked into the literature first described in chapter 2.

The development of the composite cloud

This process was first described in chapter 5 (Fig. 5.4). The step from having a set of clouds drawn from a range of differing situations, people and environments to one single cloud that encompasses the set is relatively straightforward and was described in chapter 5. Examining each box in the cloud in turn, and bearing in mind the questions, which each box contains, what is being sought is a single statement which captures the statements in each individual corresponding box in the various clouds. In each of the clouds of chapter 5 the people involved highlighted both their frustration and their desire to achieve something significant. Examination of their clouds revealed that in almost all cases they had a clear goal in mind, either related to the organisation or to their own personal development in either careers or organisational terms. This can then be placed in the **A** box of the composite cloud. This is shown once more in Fig. 6.1.

The next step is to repeat this for each box in the individual clouds. It is important to try to identify the threads that may pass through most or all of the clouds collected rather than to try and examine each one in turn. In this way the **C** box concentrated on attempting to deal with organisational blockages and problems in order to achieve the goal as written in the **A** box. For example, the cloud in Fig. 5.5 suggests working as a team,

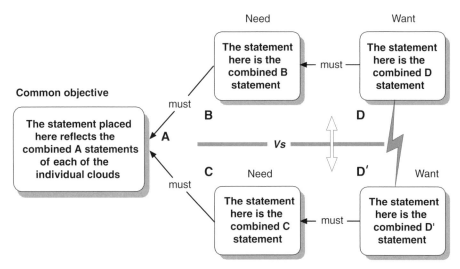

Fig. 6.1. The construction of the composite cloud

while the one in Fig. 5.13 expresses the need for delivering the targets set as the requirement for achieving the goal. The entries in the **D** box and the **D′** box were all driven by the conflicts felt by each of those participating in the research and the common thread was initially suggested as being the conflict between not changing in **D** and changing in **D′**.

The problem lay in what to place in the **B** box. This proved to be the most difficult as those participating found it very hard to say what was preventing them from implementing the proposed solution. I took the opportunity to share this cloud at this stage with a number of people working in the same field. This was the first instance of involving other people in the analytical phase of the research. As discussed in chapter 5, an early decision of the research process was not to involve other practitioners in the same field at an early stage; rather to wait until there was a single composite cloud in existence, one which was not yet complete but sufficiently developed for valuable discussion to take place. The difficulties surrounding the phrasing of the content of the **B** box was considered to be an appropriate point for such widening of the involvement. The people invited to participate at this step complied with the assumptions outlined in the preceding chapter. They had previous knowledge and skill in the use of the cloud technique. They were familiar with the subject area of the people from whom the data was collected. They were also the people chosen to assist with the validation of the generic cloud, which will be discussed later. The people chosen were Dr Goldratt and Oded Cohen of the Avraham Y. Goldratt Institute, Prof. Alan Leader of Southern Connecticut State University, Prof. David Bergland of Iowa State University and Dr Jack DeGoia of Georgetown University, Washington DC. They were

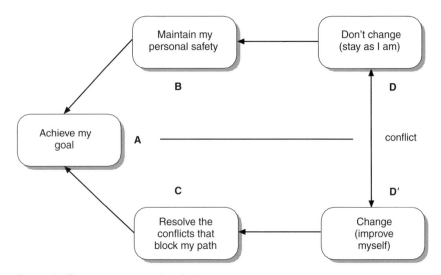

Fig. 6.2. The composite cloud (first attempt)

each invited to comment on the various suggestions for the content of the **B** box and to compare it to their own experience. The debate surrounded the need for the individual to be safe and to feel secure in their work environment. This was derived from statements such as those in Figs. 5.10, 5.11 and 5.12. This led to the first statement in the **B** box in Fig. 6.2.

Once the process of determining the entry for each box in the composite cloud was completed, the cloud was then checked by reading the logic in the manner described earlier. The strength of the cloud was also checked through the nature of the cross-connections.

The second step is the surfacing of the assumptions that lie beneath each arrow. This in turn checks the logic of the cloud once more and when the statements, as written in each box, fail to capture the entities in the individual boxes, the composite cloud is rewritten and thus upgraded. In this case the entities did not quite capture the essence of what concerned the individuals. The next figure, 6.3, shows the second iteration of the composite cloud.

The cloud reads as follows

> *In order to achieve my goal in life I must break the constraints that block me, and then, in order to break the constraints that block me, I must change. However, in order to achieve my goal I must remain in/retain control and then, in order to remain/retain control I must stay as I am.*

The logic of the cloud is as follows. The individual knows that there is a goal to be achieved. One necessary condition for the achievement of that goal is the need to break the constraints that block the way forward. In

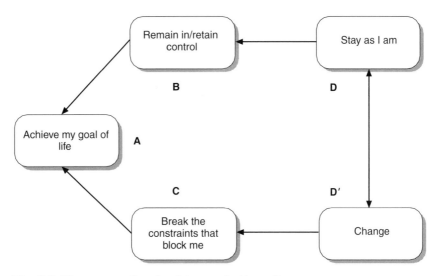

Fig. 6.3. The composite cloud (second attempt)

certain cases this will involve personal change. The change may be in what is done, the responsibilities assumed, the actions that are necessary and so on. However, the change is seen by the individual as a threat to the other necessary condition, that written in the box **B** of the cloud. The logic is that if the individual has to change then control is lost. That cannot be countenanced and therefore the change does not take place. The next step of surfacing assumptions was carried out focusing in particular on the arrow **B–D**, as this is the arrow that should be focused on, with the result as shown in Fig. 6.4.

The key issue that arose out of this analysis was that the current para-digms of the individual, what Argyris (1992) calls the 'governing variables' and what Checkland (1981) calls 'W', were key factors in governing the decision-making process of the individual, especially when considering change which affected them personally. In each of the clouds of chapter 5, the current paradigms of the individuals were effectively locking them into the *status quo* thus preventing the proposed change from taking place.

What the composite cloud was demonstrating was the ability to verba-lise this locking of the individual into their current paradigm. This led to the description of the composite cloud as the *paradigm lock cloud*. Once the cloud had been verbalised in this way, it was possible to return to both the data collected and some of the people involved checking whether this cloud captured their predicament. This led to the final step, which was to examine whether this apparently dysfunctional, irrational behaviour, on the part of the individual, all of which was giving rise to the inactivity and defensive behaviours they exhibited, could be explained by the

121

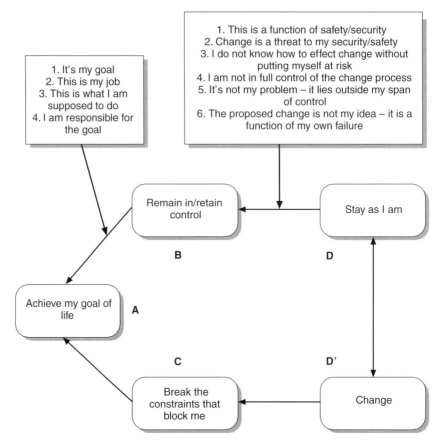

Fig. 6.4. Assumptions related to the composite cloud

paradigm lock cloud. This analysis led to the final iteration of the cloud as shown in Fig. 6.5.

The personal paradigm is simply defined as the set of values or beliefs that the individual holds about a particular subject hence 'with respect to' contained within the boxes **D** and **D′**. It might be about cost accounting, it might be about production scheduling, it might be about any area where some change is required. The key element is that the individual holds this set of values and is not minded to change them. For each of the people in chapter 5 there were many areas of their lives where change was not an issue or a blockage. However, when the proposed change was seen by the individual to significantly threaten a personal paradigm then the lock came into play. They often knew that change has to take place. They had, in this research, been involved in both the analysis of the original problem and the development of the solution. However, come the moment of implementation, when no other avenue was open to them, the full power of the lock was activated.

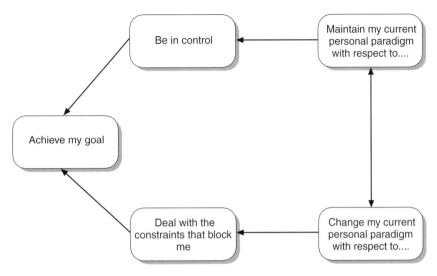

Fig. 6.5. The paradigm lock cloud

Linking the paradigm lock cloud (PLC) to the case studies

Given that the PLC had been derived from the data collected as part of the case studies, this next stage required that the new cloud be checked against those who had taken part. Also, as an extension of this validation process, the cloud and the process of construction should be exposed to other practitioners active in the same field. Therefore validation followed two distinct avenues. The first was returning to many who had taken part in the original data collection and inviting them to consider what had been developed and to relate it to their own environment. The clouds were presented to them and observations invited. This process proved to be reasonably successful in that although not all were able to return to the review and validation process, those who did participated without hesitation. The communication of each cloud followed the same path. First, they were invited to comment on the conflict they had themselves experienced. Once this was confirmed, they were asked to examine the composite cloud and the resulting generic cloud. They were asked first whether the new cloud was clear to them. Secondly, whether it was relevant to them personally. Of the seven people that took part in this section of the validation all supported both the generic cloud and the impact it had on them personally.

Of course not all that took part in the research were able to complete this activity and for subsequent research it may be more appropriate to ensure that all those people whose clouds are used for the construction of the composite cloud are able to validate the outcome of the analysis.

123

However, based on those who did take part, this validation exercise led to confirmation that the PLC was a clear verbalisation of the internal conflict they had felt at the time. For further research, more time could be given to assessing the generic cloud in conjunction with all those who had taken part. This could be done through electronic media such as the Internet. Any method that reduces the time involvement of the researcher will add to this element of validation.

Gaining a level of confidence in the applicability of the cloud to the original data set is one thing, checking whether it applies to a new, wider set is another. The second element of validation involved the use of other practitioners in the field. The importance of peer review is vital in this type of research. Once more the opportunity to show the cloud to others was taken, the initial group being those involved in the earlier stage of determining the content of box **B**. They were chosen, first, because of their skill and knowledge of TOC and the use of clouds in particular. Second, they were chosen as they had access through their own university departments to more potential candidates for the research. In other words they had their own group of people who could test both the cloud and the process of obtaining the data. As they were experienced in the use of clouds it was expected that they would have similar skills in pattern recognition, a role which is vital if the creation of the composite cloud is to be readily achieved. Finally, it was thought that they would have the necessary time to devote themselves to this activity.

They were each asked three questions. First, could they, from a group of people to which they have access, determine that there is this blockage, this obstacle to successful change, which lies at the heart of this research? Second, could they build the individual clouds of each person that meets this criteria and then build a composite cloud? Third, having built their own composite cloud, could they compare it to the one proposed within this research and respond with their results?

There are problems associated with the approach adopted for validation. First, there is the question of whether those asked would have the necessary time to carry out the validation. The second is whether they have, at the time of asking, a group they can use as a potential source of data. The people chosen all met the criteria set in chapter 5 and it is clear that without the required level of skill in the use of the cloud technique, it would be very difficult to replicate the original study. Indeed time itself is a problem as to date only one of those asked has been able to respond, which is dealt with in chapter 7. Some have given feedback in private, which suggests that they have found similar instances of conflict leading to implementations being stopped, or not started at all. They suggest that the PLC is operating within the environments they are investigating but it is too early to accept this data as validation. What cannot be avoided is that there is a requirement for anyone seeking to validate this research to have a good working knowledge of TOC and clouds.

Linking the paradigm lock cloud to models of change

In chapter 2 a simple model of change was described. Given the determination of a clearly verbalised obstacle in the form of the PLC the next step was to review the model in the light of the cloud. The original model consisted of four stages, which were now seen as insufficient to describe the processes taking place. This led to the first extension of the original model to that shown in Fig. 6.6.

Through this expansion, the increased level of detail highlighted, with greater clarity, the stages of problem solving. One element was still missing, namely, that in many cases the model did not proceed past stage 5, solution implementation. Indeed often no implementation took place at all. It was this factor that had led to the description of the PLC as one source of non-completion. Noting this omission led to the next enhancement of the change model as shown in Fig. 6.7. This shows the change process surrounding the implementation stage in more detail and in particular the arrow under which the PLC acts.

It should be noted that there were occasions when problems did occur, but they fell into the category of a rational or functional explanation for the non-performance. In those cases the people involved simply returned to the part of the process that required further work and carried it out and then moved to a successful conclusion. Examples of these included

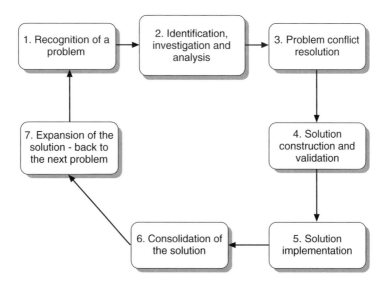

Fig. 6.6. First review of the change model

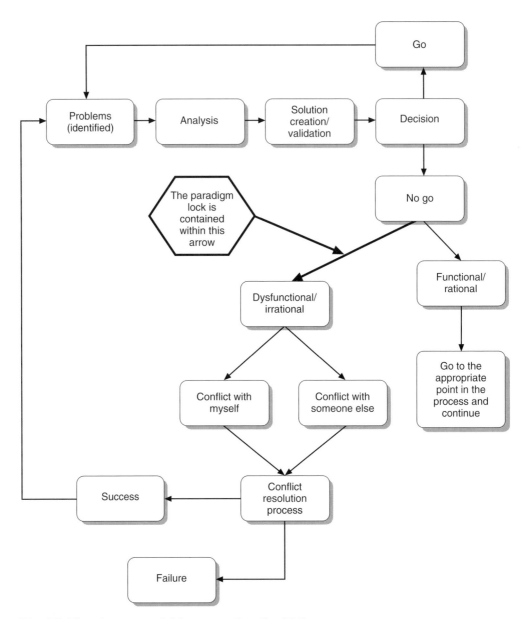

Fig. 6.7. The change model incorporating the PLC

times when the original analysis was found to be wanting in some respect, perhaps inadequate analysis of the market, or poor product development. In other cases it was the recognition that the problems being addressed were in fact not the correct or the most urgent ones and this forced those involved to return to an earlier stage on the model and re-evaluate their work and possibly change tack altogether. These reasons for not progressing with the implementation were seen as rational. However, this research has shown that there is also an irrational, dysfunctional force operating that prevents the implementations taking place. This led to the revision of the change model to include that factor. For this research, the key area of analysis was that shown by the thick line in Fig. 6.7.

The obstacle to change first considered in chapter 1 and developed in the research questions of chapter 3 is the paradigm lock cloud acting at the point shown in a change process.

The impact of the paradigm lock cloud on the individual

People for whom this acts as an obstacle feel that there is no way out of their situation. The logical effects in terms of outcomes of their situation are very clear; often the causal relationships behind the logic are not.

If they are involved in attacking a problem it is reasonable to assume that some form of change will have to take place. Where the change does not affect a personal paradigm the individual has no difficulty in accepting the proposed change, it simply takes place. Where the proposed change violates a personal paradigm then the PLC begins to take effect. Decisions, which can be made in line with the personal paradigm, are relatively simple to make, those, which undermine the personal paradigm, become extremely difficult. If it is possible, then the decision to go ahead with the change is postponed. If this is not possible, then other delaying tactics are brought into play. Hence the personal paradigm becomes a barrier to change, which leaves the individual unable to deal with the original problem or constraint. This in turn means that the original goal, written in box **A**, cannot be achieved, because dealing with the problem/constraint is a necessary condition. This leaves only what is written in box **B** as the goal of the individual. Within the case studies many involved found that their primary purpose at work was to protect their personal paradigm.

Conclusions

This chapter set out to develop the composite cloud from those collected during the research. Just using those described in chapter 5 produced a composite cloud, which was then developed into a generic cloud known as the Paradigm Lock Cloud. The impact of the cloud on the change process itself was identified by examining the change model first described in chapter 2 and further developed here. This led to the primary finding of this research that the cloud known as Paradigm Lock Cloud lies behind the behaviour pattern of those tasked with change but who fail to do so in a dysfunctional, irrational manner. They were trapped in a W of such power, a governing variable of such importance to them personally, that any other option was not allowed. The obstacle to change which started this research, and which forms the core of the research questions is this cloud.

CHAPTER SEVEN

Developing conclusions from the research

Introduction

The research set out to determine why implementation projects, mainly in manufacturing companies, fail even when the analysis of the problem and the development of the solution and the implementation plan seem to have been properly dealt with. Access to a group of people tasked with such projects was negotiated at the outset of the research phase and led to the collection of data in the form of clouds.

In chapter 3 the research problem was defined in the form of three research questions. The first was,

> *Can the block to improvement which is by definition dysfunctional, be identified?*

The second was,

> *Can the block be verbalised in a clear and logical fashion in such a way that allows for proper analysis of the block?*

Finally, the third question asked,

> *Is it possible to verbalise the block in such a way that it is possible to determine the necessary actions that must be taken in order to remove the block?*

The data collection focused on the first two questions initially and led to the creation of the paradigm lock cloud (PLC). This is the block as suggested in the first two questions, and through the use of the cloud technique allows for a proper analysis of the block.

Following the ability to develop the PLC, the relationship of that cloud to the current, ruling paradigm of the individual was clear. The framework outlined in chapter 3 was found to be the case in those examples cited in chapter 5. Further studies carried out in the UK and described later in this chapter, also support the nature of the framework and the impact of the PLC. Therefore the area of dysfunctional, irrational behaviour highlighted by the arrow in Fig. 6.7 is the area where the PLC is most active and acts as a barrier to change.

As the PLC identified in chapter 6 is considered to be a sound articulation of the barrier to change which was first raised in chapter 1 and discussed in more detail in chapter 3, then it follows that it should be overcome. If this obstacle exists then it can be safely assumed that no real improvement can take place until it has been overcome.

This chapter then is concerned with a number of critical issues. The first is a return to the question of validity first raised in chapter 6. This is primarily a question of the internal validity of the research process. The second element of validity is the question of replaceability. Can the process described be used by others? What are the parameters of such use and what results have been obtained to date, if any? This chapter also contains a clear statement of the contribution to knowledge as a result of this study. Other discussion points examine the possible approaches to deal with the removal of the paradigm lock and reflect on further areas of research. In particular the setting of the paradigm lock cloud into a sequence of clouds that affect change programmes and a structured approach to implementing change.

Validation of the research process

There are two key areas of validity. The first is the level of validity that can be accorded to the process that I used. This entails an analysis of the process used and a consideration given to the question as to why the process seems to work in producing the results gained. The types of questions include the ability to set boundaries for the research, checking the appropriateness of the chosen approach and the lessons learned. The second area of validity is external. Can someone else replicate the study and the results of the research described here? This is an important dimension in terms of the replication of results but also the confidence that can be gained in the research process itself.

Validity of the research

When it comes to determining the method for research the criteria set by Bouchard (1976) was 'asking the right question and picking the most powerful method for answering that particular question'. The choice of method was determined by the specific nature of the set of questions described in chapter 3. As they concerned an hypothesis that had at its core a series of elements that were hidden from view, the method had to be capable of questioning and checking causality. This need to check behind initial responses led to the requirement of active participation of the researcher.

Equally, there was a recognition that the approach must deliver verifiable results, capable of test and replicability. This was very much in line with Kerlinger (1973) and his argument that science sets out to explain what is happening, the explanation being termed a theory. Thus the research focused on a qualitative study due in large part to the need to determine the causal factors that exist within the lives of the people participating, how they function within the organisation, and how they interact. It was felt that quantitative methods would not be able to produce the richness of data, or the explicit causal connections sought after as part of the research questions.

Thus the process led naturally to qualitative methods developing a series of case studies. It also meant that the case studies would be developed in real-time in the field. This allowed me to check progress and to change the way in which the involvement of the individuals was achieved. The intention of this was to discover the significant variables pertaining to the research and to discover relationships between them. This active participation of myself, clearly in the role of a participant observer, and the research itself, took the study into the field of action research.

As a result of this it was plain that there is a necessity for my role to be clear. At what point is the research the prime activity and when is it not? Confusion in the mind of the respondent is a clear danger without such clarification of roles. The need to have such clarification was clear from the outset. The negotiation with the respondent was undertaken at the earliest point. Every stage of data collection was clearly identified with the respondents in advance.

The data collection also involved the use of a specific tool – the cloud. Were the respondents not to understand what was required of both them and the technique there could well be a danger of dissonance, of detachment from the study. The active participation of the respondents was fundamental, as was their need to be honest to both themselves and the researcher. Therefore the use of the tool had to be demonstrated to the respondents. They had to recognise what the tool was trying to achieve. Here the role of the researcher/practitioner is vital. His knowledge of the tool, and the ability to create empathy is a core element of this aspect of data collection. Creating the right environment where people feel they can open up and be candid is what had to be achieved from the outset. This required me to have that ability to put people at ease and allow them time to discuss difficult issues without pressure. Often the time to collect one cloud would be spread over a number of sessions with each individual.

Once the data had been collected it was checked by inviting the respondents to verify what they had said by examining the clouds as written. The fact that each cloud was written down significantly aided understanding and verification. They were able to correct any statements they felt did not capture the true nature of the conflict they were experiencing. This ability to correct what was written gave them confidence in both what they were saying and in myself. It was clearly accepted that I was faithfully recording the clouds. This proved to be a major element in the robustness of the clouds collected. It is also very much in line with Hartley's (1995, in Cassell and Symon) observation that the key feature of such case studies is 'the emphasis on understanding processes as they occur in their context'.

The study followed the format developed by Grant (1996), which was, first diagnosis, second action plan, third action taken and then evaluation followed by learning. The diagnosis was the hypothesis stage and the development of the research question and data collection method. The second and third were the actual phases of data collection and analysis.

The final two stages, evaluation and learning, are still on-going even now some three years after the data collection process was completed. The evaluation stage led to the creation of the PLC and subsequent external validation of the hypothesis. Apart from the elements already discussed it also includes the ability to develop pattern recognition when moving to the creation of the composite cloud.

Learning is what this chapter is about but also other areas of further research outlined later in this chapter. Above all, learning is about the contribution to knowledge. As with action research a key element of this study was to determine working solutions to a problem identified.

This research set out to determine the nature of the obstacles to change. In Fig. 6.7 a model was produced as a result of the data collected. For this research to have validity the test lies in the ability to challenge the model through rigorous analysis and replicability. This being a human activity system as defined by Checkland (1981) there are many facets of the people and the circumstances that were not captured. The question is whether what was captured is sufficient to sustain the results. Checkland reminds us that what are collected are 'mental constructs, not would-be accounts of reality'. People felt that they faced a major obstacle in their implementation. This obstacle is a function of many aspects not all collected as part of the research. This raises the question of 'good enough'. Is the data collected and the subsequent analysis leading to the creation of the generic cloud good enough? Given the time allocated to data collection and the spread of people taking part there is certainly a reasonable size to the data group. The number of people taking part meant that there were a considerable number of clouds to form the core data set. That these clouds were also drawn from a wide section of companies, and levels within those companies, adds to the credibility that can be attached to the data set. The research therefore included a significant number of people, with a number of clouds from each of them. Although more clouds could have been added it was found that further clouds did not change the nature of the core cloud at this point. Of course further data acquisition could add clarity to this statement but this was currently beyond the scope and timescale of the research.

External validation of the research

During the time given to writing the thesis, Oded Cohen of the Avraham Y. Goldratt Institute was pursuing analysis into the PLC and trying to determine whether he could replicate the work already described here. He was one of the people chosen to both scrutinise the composite cloud construction and to validate the research itself. He is a skilled practitioner with TOC and clouds. He submitted, following a lengthy discussion with the researcher, the following four clouds. The background to the clouds is that Cohen is one of a group of people within the UK responsible for the introduction of the TOC to UK organisations and therefore has access to people who meet the criteria outlined earlier. In this case Cohen derived the clouds from a group of people seeking to teach the TOC. There is a requirement that such teaching takes both the student and the tutor towards their respective goals. The goal of the Institute is 'to generate and disseminate knowledge, which brings results' and knowledge is defined as that which brings benefit to the user. In examining the performance of tutors, Cohen developed the three clouds and then modified them using the process contained within this research to develop a composite cloud. He then compared his composite cloud to that evolved within chapter 6 and the PLC itself. The first cloud is shown in Fig. 7.1.

This cloud centred on the perceived need to avoid upsetting or giving offence to students when validating their work and giving feedback. It is the cloud of the tutors Cohen was working with at the time. The cloud was proving to be a significant obstacle for the tutor trying to make a contribution to the knowledge acquisition of their students. The tutors felt that if they gave feedback they might do so in a manner likely to cause more problems. They felt that they did not have the confidence to use the process expected of them, the TOC/TP, and that therefore they were compromised in their role as tutors.

The second cloud (Fig. 7.2) was also derived from the same group of people as the previous cloud. This was seen as a function of the conflict they felt between, on the one hand, trying to achieve what they had set out to achieve and at the same time trying to accept the reality of their

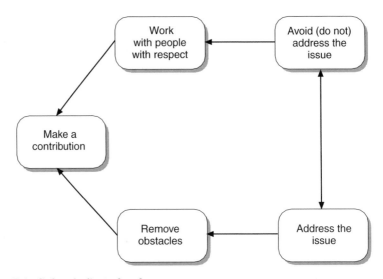

Fig. 7.1. Cohen's first cloud

current position. The conflict arose primarily because they did not set out the necessary conditions to achieve their goals. The need to belong, in this case to a specific network of colleagues, often led them to give up what they really wanted to do in their lives.

This cloud (Fig. 7.3), the final one of the set of three from the tutors, is about the methods used in teaching TOC/TP through a Socratic approach. Many of the people coming to learn about the TOC/TP, the focal point of the work Cohen and the tutors were involved in, centres on the need to

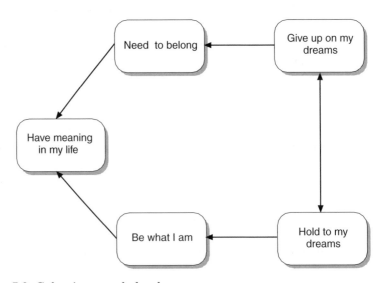

Fig. 7.2. Cohen's second cloud

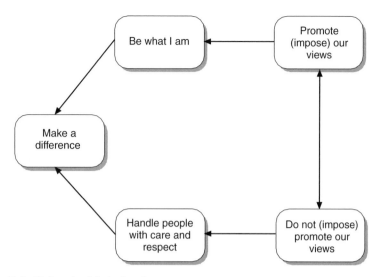

Fig. 7.3. Cohen's third cloud

use the terminology of the students rather than that of the TOC/TP. The intention is to use the Socratic approach, which starts with the use of questions where the assumption is that the person being questioned already knows the answer. Then follows the need to time the questions and ensure that the language used in the question is that of the person being asked to give the answer. Cohen found that in some cases this requirement of the Socratic approach was creating a conflict between demonstrating confidence in the use of TOC/TP and the application being considered, and showing a grasp of the students' own environment. Teaching through the use of the Socratic approach involves avoiding quite clearly the imposition of views from the tutor. Students must learn by having the knowledge developed from within themselves. Being unable to deal with this properly led to the creation of the third cloud.

Given these three clouds, and following the same path as the researcher, Cohen produced the composite cloud shown in Fig. 7.4.

This cloud captures many of the same issues that are determined in the PLC of chapter 6. Once more the lock is in evidence in that by holding to **D** and not moving to **D'** they are unable to deal with **C**: 'Handle people with care and respect'. This leads to the recognition that they are unable to achieve the goal: 'Make a difference'. This leaves them with staying as they are, in other words, 'Being what I am' with no obvious opportunity to change. The importance of subordinating themselves and what they want to do is in line with the statement in the **D** box of the PLC, which is 'Maintain my personal paradigm with respect to...'. If they shift to the subordination to the group they will consider that they are likely to lose control, the requirement written in the **B** box of the PLC. In this

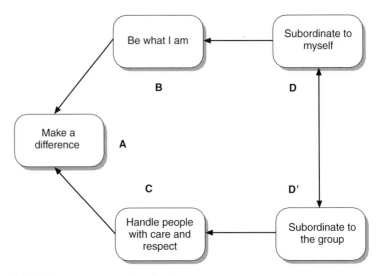

Fig. 7.4. Cohen's composite cloud

way Cohen has identified the same obstacle as that proposed, and verbalised, within this research.

Contribution to knowledge

The research set out to answer the questions first raised in chapter 3. These questions focused on the reasons why the change process in manufacturing organisations stalled. In particular the causality that exists under the arrow of Fig. 6.7 under which the paradigm lock is deemed to exist. The study identified a number of conflicts, which a group of people from manufacturing companies experienced while trying to implement change. It is not the nature or the existence of the conflicts that constitutes the primary contribution to knowledge.

The primary contribution to knowledge is the use of the evaporating cloud technique to both verbalise these conflicts and to use the technique to develop understanding about the nature of the conflict. It also created a picture of the environment in which it exists, a contextual dimension to the cloud, and set out to gain the consensus of the person with the individual conflict that it represents a clear obstacle to the change process they are attempting to implement.

Using the technique known an 'evaporating clouds', part of the process tools of the TOC/TP, a number of these conflicts were captured. The technique attempts to verbalise the conflict the individual is experiencing in a clear and understandable way. These clouds, individually, captured a specific conflict that the individual was experiencing at the time. Using the questions contained within each of the five boxes of the cloud structure, covered in chapter 4, the full cloud was obtained. Through the use of this process, based on the logic of necessity, the conflict so defined allows the individual to understand the impact of the conflict on themselves and on what they are trying to achieve.

The collection of this data involved the active participation of the researcher. Asking the questions contained in each box and seeking clarity of the answers given in order to fully understand the true nature of the conflict was an important step in the process. The clarity was gained by asking questions concerning the statements offered by the individuals and ensuring a clear verbalisation of their answers. Having accomplished the task of verbalising the conflicts it was then found possible to understand the causality of the conflict through the surfacing of the assumptions that lies beneath each arrow of the cloud. This made the conflict very visible to the individual and its impact. They could challenge the logic of the cloud, a process that enhanced the understanding in each case.

A process of integration, carried out by the researcher followed this, in order to produce one composite cloud, which encapsulated the individual clouds collected. This process centred on the ability of myself in this context, to recognise patterns of behaviour in each of the clouds and to then build that pattern into a single statement.

Once the composite cloud was developed I then returned to some of the individuals and asked them to check the wording of this new cloud and to compare it to their own circumstance. This active participation of both myself and the respondents provided the necessary confidence in the robustness of the composite cloud. At this point the cloud was considered to be a generic cloud on conflict associated with the implementation of change. Going to new respondents to determine whether they have experienced the same generic conflict further validated the existence of this cloud. This too proved successful, although the results are not included within this study.

Overcoming the paradigm lock

One of the basic assumptions of this research is that the people taking part were keen to improve the performance of their organisation. Indeed in many cases they were the driving forces for the improvement project. This was nearly always reflected in the way they suggested what was written in box **A** of their various clouds. It was also accepted that change would be a part of the solution. They accepted and understood that they could not achieve what they wanted without change, that dealing with constraints to improve performance carried with it a requirement for change. It also became clear that many of those taking part wanted to work in a safety zone where they felt confident of what they were doing and did not feel threatened in any way. This is a measure of their self-perception, and was reflected in what they wrote in the **B** box. This is very much in line with what Argyris and Schon (1996) call the 'governing variables' and what Checkland (1981) calls 'W'. The main difference here is that while both Argyris and Checkland identified that there were forces at play in the decision-making process used by people, and that in some cases these forces worked in favour of and in some cases against what was being proposed, they did not clearly verbalise the force, which prevented successful change.

This research developed their work and took it to the stage of identification of that force which leads to an understanding of the obstacle, which led to the dysfunctional/irrational failure to implement. They did not capture the real nature of this obstacle. Whatever is written in the **B** box is seen as a function of the control the individual needs within his or her life. The ability to stay in control is seen as central by those taking part in the research. The importance of this is made highly significant when a proposed change is seen to threaten that level of control. The proposed change may be rooted in powerful, compelling logic but the threat to the individual, real or imaginary, is even greater. This is the nub of the paradigm lock. The individual feels trapped with no possibility of escape. It follows that if improvement is to take place then this obstacle must be overcome. It must be done in a way that allows for the constraint to be fully and properly dealt with, and at the same time allows the individual to retain control.

As the technique to verbalise this conflict is a cloud, then it follows that the process of surfacing assumptions will enable those which are erroneous to be identified and dealt with. The primary area on which to focus attention would be the arrow **B–D** of the PLC. Recognising that this is a generic cloud leads to the conclusion that any erroneous assumptions surfaced here will probably be generic in nature. For each individual there will also be assumptions unique to that person and therefore any analysis undertaken to determine the way forward will have to take note of both generic assumptions and specific ones related to that individual. For the purposes of this research no attempt has been made to surface generic assumptions from each person. However, before the process of surfacing assumptions can be considered three factors stood out from the research.

As noted in chapter 5 and also shown on Fig. 6.7 there were people for whom this cloud did not exist. They were able to implement change even when they themselves had to change what they were doing. In examining those who were not affected by the cloud three factors were clear. The first was that each of them was able to fully subordinate what they were doing in order to achieve the goal. Whatever was written in box **A** was very much more important than anything that might have been written in box **B**. They recognised the importance of the goal, the objective, as it related to their own aspirations. They accepted that the obstacle was of greater significance to the organisation and that even though they felt certain aspects to be important to themselves, they always came second to achieving the goal. In other words they were able to subordinate themselves to the goal, or objective, of the organisation.

The second factor was that they were prepared to take responsibility, and be accountable for the results of their actions. They did not seek to apportion blame if things went wrong; they simply went back to the solution and improved it. They recognised and accepted that they were part of the problem and also part of the solution. They were already prepared to undergo the type of paradigm shift that is necessary for real change to take place.

The third factor was that they were prepared to both give and respond to leadership. They might be ready and able to give leadership, but even though they might be the top person, they were still ready to accept ideas and suggestions from any level, and act on them. The combination of these three factors gave confidence that change would take place leading to a successful conclusion of the implementation. One area of further research will be to examine these factors in greater detail and to then make a comparison between those who are successful and those who are not. At this point in time the three factors described here seem to offer a way forward in overcoming the PLC.

Returning to the analysis of the PLC the cloud is shown once more in Fig. 7.5.

This cloud still represents the current verbalisation of the barrier to change represented by the paradigm lock. It may change with more research, it may become more powerful as others build on what has been described here. What is clear is that since the research was completed I have carried out many more analyses of people within organisations and found the cloud to gain in substance and power every time. This cloud is still a very good verbalisation of one of the dysfunctional barriers to change within organisations today.

Having gained confidence in the construction of the cloud the surfacing of assumptions follows. What is shown in Fig. 7.6 came from a combination of analysis with the people taking part and subsequent analysis by both myself, and others within the TOC community. The assumptions are not as comprehensive as they might be, but they are real and tell a story.

This is not an exhaustive list of assumptions. For any one person there will be more, some of these might apply, some might not, and there will always be some specific to the individual.

139

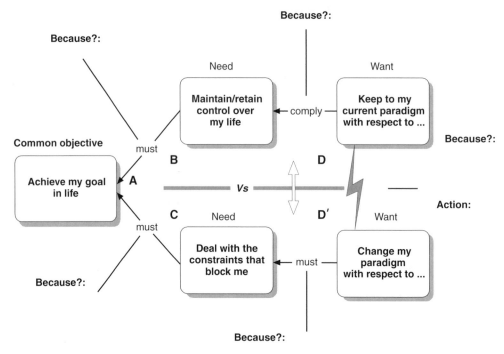

Fig. 7.5. The PLC cloud

What do these assumptions tell us? Well, bearing in mind the three factors identified above, they allow us to examine which might be erroneous
and which are true. They allow us to consider whether the three factors
overcome any of the assumptions and thus break the dependency of the
conflict.

Some additional aspects of the research process and some questions still to be answered

Other questions, which form areas for more research, include whether the
lock, if identified, can be broken before it has any negative effects on the
improvement process. Would the same results be obtained if the level of
active participation were reduced with the researcher merely observing
and analysing without the involvement of the people being studied?
Although the time taken to collect the data was extensive, the question
of time is still relevant. Can the results be obtained in a shorter time
scale? The feedback from the others attempting to replicate this study,
and discussed earlier in this chapter, suggests that the same problems
were experienced. They are now examining the results of this research
with the additional element of setting their analysis into a structured
approach to implementations.

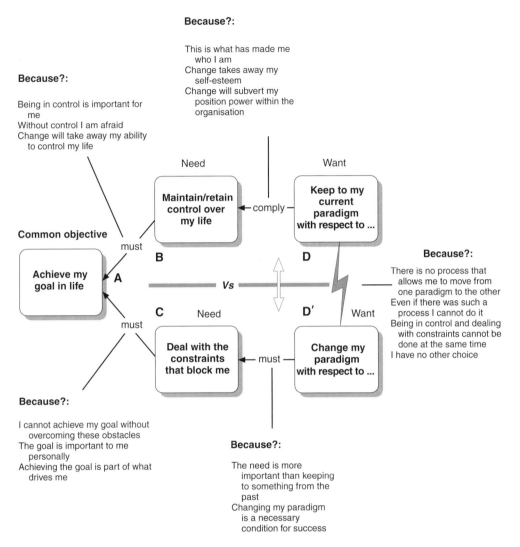

Because?:

This is what has made me
who I am
Change takes away my
self-esteem
Change will subvert my
position power within the
organisation

Because?:

Being in control is important for
me
Without control I am afraid
Change will take away my ability
to control my life

Need

Want

**Maintain/retain
control over
my life** ←comply→ **Keep to my
current
paradigm
with respect to ...**

Common objective

must

B

D

**Achieve my
goal in life** A

Vs

Because?:

There is no process that
allows me to move from
one paradigm to the other
Even if there was such a
process I cannot do it
Being in control and dealing
with constraints cannot be
done at the same time
I have no other choice

C Need D′ Want

must

**Deal with the
constraints
that block me** ← must → **Change my
paradigm
with respect to ...**

Because?:

I cannot achieve my goal without
overcoming these obstacles
The goal is important to me
personally
Achieving the goal is part of what
drives me

Because?:

The need is more
important than keeping
to something from the
past
Changing my paradigm
is a necessary
condition for success

Fig. 7.6. The assumptions of the paradigm lock cloud

The five stages of successful implementation

Part of what this research identified was related to other work being
carried out by the Avraham Y. Goldratt Institute and myself in terms of
a process of implementation. The Goldratt Institute described this process
in terms of 'layers of resistance'. I prefer to use a more pro-active term –
the five steps of successful change. This was described in more detail in
Hutchin (2001) *Enterprise-focused management.*

Step 1 – *Consensus on the problem.* This means that the people tasked
with improving the performance of their organisation agree on the nature

of the problem and the impact it is having on the organisation. They may have used a structured logical process to achieve this level of agreement, or come to the conclusion through their own intuition. The important element is the level of consensus achieved.

Step 2 – *Consensus on the direction of the solution*. This means that the broad direction of the solution is agreed. There are few details of the actual solution, merely an outline that gives the people concerned enough to recognise that if implemented this solution will deal with the problem agreed in the first phase.

Step 3 – *Consensus on the benefits of the solution*. This is where the full solution is developed and tested. It may involve rigorous analysis of the proposed benefits or it may involve the use of outside consultants to validate the solution. What is clear is that the solution is checked prior to implementation.

Step 4 – *Dealing with all the possible reservations people might have about the proposal*. These include the potential negative outcomes of the solution: this is where the people involved bring the input from many others within the organisation in order to check for potential negative outcomes, should the implementation proceed. Again the process used is less important than the checking of the solution against the intuition of the people within the organisation. It is also about dealing with the obstacles to prevent the implementation taking place – this is where the obstacles to the implementation itself are debated and dealt with. It is part of the process that every obstacle must be overcome if the implementation is to be completed successfully.

Step 5 – *Making it happen*. If all the preceding phases have been accomplished then there is nothing to prevent the solution being implemented. It is at this point that the paradigm lock is considered to become effective in the prevention of implementations.

One further aspect of this study raises the existence of levels of clouds leading to the paradigm lock. Following the research, I developed the concept that there are three levels of clouds operating in a clear hierarchy. The first level is that of a decision cloud. This cloud is about the decision to implement a particular solution. The decision therefore is between two opposing approaches each purporting to deal with the problem under review. The debate that takes place prior to the decision appears to focus on the merits of each proposed solution rather than the ability of the solution to properly deal with the problem. It is this debate that gives rise to the existence of the cloud.

The second level is that of a conflict of subordination cloud. Here the decision that led to the existence of the first level cloud, the decision cloud, has been taken. The assumption now is that the people within the organisation will subordinate to the decision and implement it. This research suggested that this is not always the case and there were times when people said they would support an implementation and then failed to do so when required. There could be many reasons for non-compliance with the implementation, some of which could be perfectly reasonable such as a decision to not proceed due to a change in the market or a change in the management structure. Whatever the causality for non-compliance these issues present themselves as valid areas of possible research. Hand (MBA unpublished thesis 2001) has researched this area in some detail and has confirmed both the impact that conflict of subordination can have, and also that this cloud does not necessarily lead to the paradigm lock cloud.

However, the main thrust of this research has shown that for some people the proposed implementation becomes a threat to their current paradigm. This leads to the third level of clouds – the paradigm lock cloud.

The TOC/TP itself is subject to on-going examination and improvement. The research focused on the use of the TOC/TP with respect to managers within manufacturing. The issues raised by the research are not unique to manufacturing but to any manager or indeed any person trying to achieve a goal. This raises one final question for consideration in terms of further research. If the TOC/TP is a generic tool for problem solving then it should work for any problem. This research examined problems generated in the manufacturing environment, however, they could equally be raised in another environment. The clouds of chapter 5 are not exclusively about manufacturing, they are about relationships between people. They are also about how people feel about themselves and their own goals in life. Perhaps the real power of these tools lies in the ability of the individual to develop a personal focus about what they want to achieve in their lives and how to do it. These questions are already being raised and work has already started to develop TOC/TP in this way, but that goes beyond the scope of this research taking it into the realm of psychology and psycho-dynamics.

Final thoughts about the research process

The area of action research is one that continues to raise questions about the dependability of the results and the possible impact the researcher has on the group being studied. It would have been more difficult to obtain both the quantity and quality of the data without the access offered. During the research period the researcher was playing an active role with each participant in addition to the research itself. This had the advantage of allowing a clear and honest relationship to develop which encouraged those being studied to open up and share secrets that might otherwise not surface.

The clouds described in chapter 5 were the result of a considerable effort by the researcher in gaining the trust and confidence of the people concerned. The emotions raised by these clouds go deep, yet lie at the heart of the change process. It was essential to encourage people to share these feelings and emotions and to help them verbalise issues that were, in some circumstances, hurting them personally. It is doubtful that these results could have been obtained without the active participation of the researcher.

However, it was recognised that the very level of active involvement can itself lead to a lack of detached and objective assessment. Recognising that this is an issue goes some way to ensuring that it does not become a major problem. Any process that involves active participation will, by definition, raise these issues. For this research a distinction was made when working with the people concerned between the normal working relationship and the research. They chose to come to the researcher with issues that they felt were important to both the work they were doing and the research itself.

The role of the researcher in this study was clear. However, other people work in the same way with manufacturing managers. One final area of further research is to consider reducing the level of active involvement and develop the issues either through simple observation or through quantitative methods. This may itself have substantial difficulties but would go some way to address the issues raised by the approach used here.

The final observation of this research is the impact it has had on the work carried out by myself in various organisations. Through the identification of the PLC and the nature of the impact it has on the individual it has been possible to take time with implementations to ensure that the threat to the current ruling paradigm is reduced and that such implementations proceed without the problems faced within the research case studies. The research has demonstrated that it is possible to use the cloud technique to examine the ways in which people approach change and in a manner that they can readily accept.

CHAPTER EIGHT

Developing the solution to paradigm lock

This chapter contains a discussion about the next steps in the process of improvement. The paradigm lock cloud has been found in many places since the conclusion of the research period. In implementations around both Europe and the USA the same phenomenon has been determined in many different circumstances and situations.

Chapter 3 suggested that there are three further questions that need to be considered, the first relates to the necessary features of the solution required to successfully overcome the power and devastating impact of the lock. The next is how successful are these features, can they be subjected to the same level of rigour that the problem was given? Finally, are there missing features of a general nature or, for each individual, are additional features going to be determined unique to that person?

The ability to develop an implementable solution

The process of problem analysis and solution creation which is the core of the TOC approach to problem solving can be described in the following manner. Step one is to develop an implementable solution. Fig. 8.1 is read from the bottom up using the phrase 'if... then'. It is the logic of sufficiency.

Once this process has been completed there is then the question of proceeding to implementation. Here there are two distinct options, to proceed or not to proceed. Although there are many different aspects to proceeding, or not, the key factors being examined here relate to the individual rather than the organisation. Consider option 1 as shown by Fig. 8.2.

Here the proposed solution has no impact on the paradigm of the individual, even when he or she is being asked to change a paradigm, the implication here is that the end is much more important than the fact that a personal paradigm will have to change. In other words the goal, the objective, is more important than retaining the paradigm. However, this is not always the case as the research has shown. This problem is described in Fig. 8.3.

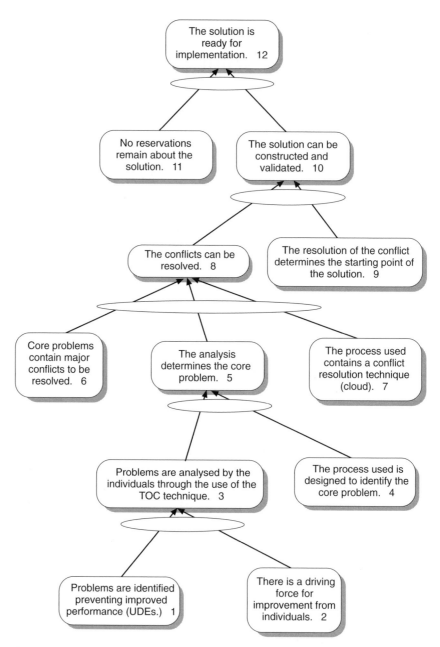

Fig. 8.1. The initial starting point

Here the impact of the paradigm lock is clear. The decision to not proceed is driven by the impact the individual sees the solution will have on their current, dominant paradigm. In order to successfully implement the original solution the paradigm lock must be overcome first. One

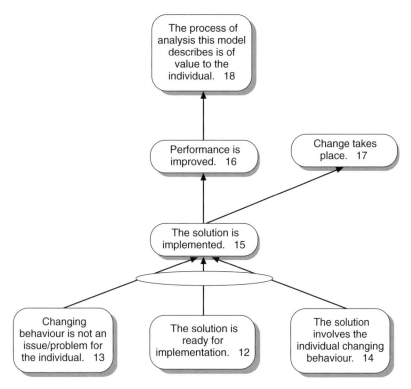

Fig. 8.2. The process when paradigms are not under threat

dimension dominates the discussion from here. It is often felt that it would be easy to overcome the paradigm lock simply by pressure, force the individual to change and be done with it. However, this violates one of my beliefs about how to manage an organisation, the intention should always be to achieve win–win and forcing the individual to change is not win–win. Some might argue that I have placed a new constraint upon management, well I see it not as a constraint but as a necessary condition for successful management. Of course there will always be times when all attempts to resolve the issue fail and hard decisions will have to be considered, but only after exhaustive attempts to help the individual overcome the lock and move forward. It should also be remembered that in that particular process we may find that some of our own assumptions are not as clear and unequivocal as we thought.

There are two dimensions to overcoming the paradigm lock, one from the individual and one from the rest of the organisation in partnership with the individual.

Dealing with the individual first, three features of the solution were developed by first analysing the successful people, those for whom changing paradigms was rarely if ever a problem. What characteristics

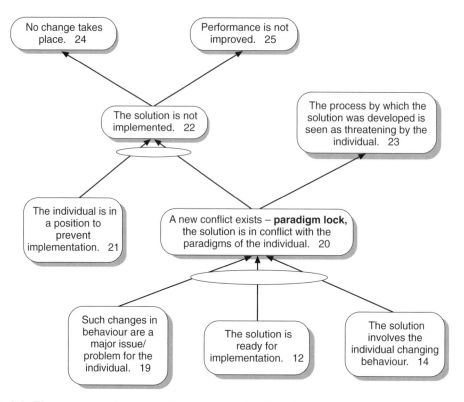

Fig. 8.3. The process when paradigms are under threat

did they exhibit when faced with implementing solutions that contained major change? The first was that they always focused on the big picture, the goal of the enterprise, and the constraints that were preventing improvement towards the goal. They had the ability to rise above the tactical issues and see the strategic issues very clearly. So this was placed as feature number one of the solution – focus, and by that I mean subordinate, allow nothing else to have a greater priority, on the goal of the organisation and the constraints preventing improvement.

The second characteristic was that these people never participated in the usual blame culture that dominates many of our organisations. They always took upon themselves the responsibility for what they had done, they knew they had to be accountable for the results of their actions and not try to pin the blame of non-performance on the markets, the customers, the other functions within the organisation, indeed anyone except themselves. Even when they were not responsible they would try to take that responsibility on and then try to do something about it. This gave rise to the second feature of the solution – that each person takes responsibility, and is accountable for the results of his or her actions.

The third characteristic became very obvious while working with the successful people, they always seemed to giving clear leadership and direction. They never shirked that responsibility. They would also listen carefully to ideas and suggestions from others no matter their position within the team. They would analyse the suggestions, and give good feedback whether they were going to proceed or not. This gave the third feature of the solution – be prepared to both give, and respond, to leadership.

These three features were common amongst the successful managers that took part in the research. But these features on their own would be insufficient to overcome the full impact of paradigm lock. This creates a person who is ready for change, but the change itself must still make sense, it must address a limitation within the organisation. This is where three other features were developed.

In order to have confidence in the solution there has to be confidence in the analytical approach used to determine both the real nature of the problem and the creation of the solution. There are three key questions that must be answered, What to change? What to change to? and How to effect the change? The process used must be capable of answering these questions. It must also be able to meet the requirements of the five steps of successful change outlined earlier, and repeated here.

- Step 1: There must be consensus on the problem throughout the team.
- Step 2: There must be consensus on the direction of the solution throughout the team.
- Step 3: There must be consensus on the benefits of the solution for all the team and the organisation as a whole.
- Step 4: All reservations must be overcome properly and to the satisfaction of those raising them.
- Step 5: Make it happen.

Therefore feature number four is the ability to use a process that can answer the three questions above and follow the steps of change. There has to be a readiness to change paradigms and that means that feature number five is about the environment created within the organisation which is all about win–win. The final feature is to be aware of the dangers of inertia. It is very easy, and comforting to continue with the *status quo*. It is clear that in many organisations the most robust state is where we are today. The most fragile is the movement to a new environment which currently only creates fear. It is the challenge of the people who read this book to unleash the potential that resides within every employee from the very top to the very bottom. Each person has the ability to make a difference, if they are allowed to do so.

Organisations can face constraints that are physical, policies or, as this book has shown, paradigms. None need remain to prevent the organisation from achieving the goal it sets out to achieve. People need not give up on their goals, they can be achieved if, and only if, other people allow them to. There is a wealth of talent and imagination captured in every organisation, many fail to release it and thus lose. This is now a self-fulfilling prophecy, it can be addressed, but it takes time, it takes cares and above all it takes thinking. To quote the title of the book by Lisa Scheinkopf, are you ready to start *Thinking for a change?*

Bibliography

Argyris C. (1990). Inappropriate defenses against the monitoring of organization development practices. *J. Applied Behavioral Science*, **26**(3), 299–312.

Argyris C. (1992). *On organizational learning*. Blackwell, Cambridge, Mass.

Argyris C. (1993). *Knowledge for action*. Jossey-Bass, San Francisco.

Argyris C. and Schon D. A. (1996). *Organizational learning II*. Addison-
Wesley, Wokingham.

Argyris C., Putnam R. and McLain Smith D. (1985). *Action science*. Jossey-
Bass, San Francisco.

Atkinson P. E. (1985). Who should manage change? *Management Services*,
29(2), 14–15.

Bach R. (1977). *Illusions*. Dell Publishing, New York.

Bennett R. (1983). *Management research*. International Labour Office,
Geneva.

Blau P. M. (1967). The hierarchy of authority in organisations. *American
journal of Sociology*, 1967–68, 453–467.

Bouchard T. J. (1976) in Dunnette M. D. (ed). *Handbook of industrial and
organisational psychology*. Rand McNally, Chicago.

Bransford J. D. and Stein B. S. (1984). *The ideal problem solver*. Freeman, New
York.

Brooks E. (1980). *Organizational change: The managerial dilemma*. Macmillan,
London.

Buchanan D. A. and Huczynski A. A. (1985). *Organisational behaviour*.
Prentice Hall International.

Burns T. and Stalker G. (1966). *The management of innovation*. Tavistock,
London.

Caruth D. L. (1974). Basic psychology. *J. Systems Management*, Feb., 10–13.

Cassell C. and Symon G. (eds) (1995). *Qualitative methods in organisational
research*. Sage, London.

Checkland P. (1981). *Systems thinking, systems practice*. John Wiley,
Chichester.

Checkland P. and Scholes J. (1990). *Soft systems methodology in action*. John
Wiley, Chichester.

Clark P. A. (1972). *Action research and organisational change*. Harper and
Row, London.

Corbett T. (1998). *Throughput accounting*. North River Press, Great Barrington,
MA.

Cox J. C. and Spencer M. S. (1998). *The constraints management handbook*.
St Lucie Press, Boca Raton.

Dalton M. (1959). *Men who manage*. Wiley, New York.

Deming W. E. (1986). *Out of the crisis*. MIT CAES, Cambridge, Mass.

Deming W. E. (1994). *The new economics*. CAES, Cambridge, Mass.

Dettmer H. W. (1997). *Goldratt's Theory of Constraints*. ASQC Quality Press, Milwaukee, Wisconsin.

Dey I. (1993). *Qualitative data analysis*. Routledge, London.

Drucker P. F. (1980). *Managing in turbulent times*. Butterworth Heinemann, London.

Easton G. (1992). *Learning from case studies*. Prentice Hall, Hemel Hempstead.

Emery F. E. (1967). The case study method. *Tavistock Report*, Doc. No. 265, Tavistock Institute of Human Relations, London.

Emery F. E. and Trist E. L. (1965). The causal texture of organizational environments. *Human Relations*, **18**, 21–32.

Etzioni A. (1964). *Modern organizations*. Prentice-Hall, New Jersey.

Feigenbaum A. V. (1991). *Total quality control*. 3rd ed., McGraw Hill, New York.

Fensham and Hooper (1964) in Emery F. E. (1967). The case study method. *Tavistock Report*, Doc. No. 265, Tavistock Institute of Human Relations, London.

Follett M. P. (1995). *Prophet of management*. Harvard Business School Press.

Gilmore M. and Smith D. J. (1996). Set-up reduction in pharmaceutical manufacturing: an action research study. *International Journal of Operations and Production Management*, **16**(3), 4–17.

Goldratt E. M. (1990a). *Theory of Constraints*. North River Press, New York.

Goldratt E. M. (1990b). *The haystack syndrome*. North River Press, London.

Goldratt E. M. (1997). *Critical chain*. North River Press, Great Barrington, MA.

Goldratt E. M. and Cox J. (1984). *The goal*. Gower, London.

Goldratt E. M. and Fox R. (1986). *The race*. North River Press, London.

Grant D. (1996). Action research as a vehicle for validating MISD methodologies. *International Journal of Computer Integrated Manufacture*, **9**(5), Sep.–Oct., 381–391.

Gummesson E. (1988). Qualitative methods in management research. Studentlitteratur, Chartwell-Brat.

Hand S. C. (2001). An analysis of the barrier to change entitled 'Conflict of Subordination'. Submitted as part of MBA at Leicester University.

Handy C. B. (1985). *Understanding organisations*. Penguin, London.

Hayes J. R. (1981). *The complete problem solver*. The Franklin Institute Press, Philadelphia.

Hayes R. H. and Wheelwright S. C. (1984). *Restoring our competitive edge*. John Wiley, London.

Hayes R. H., Wheelwright S. C. and Clark K. B. (1988). *Dynamic manufacturing*. Free Press, London.

Hersey P. and Blanchard K. H. (1972). The management of change. *Training and Development Journal*, Jan., 6–10.

Hersey P. and Blanchard K. (1988). *Management of organizational behavior*. Prentice-Hall International, New Jersey.

Hutchin C. E. (1986). Paving the way for technological change. *Proc. 3rd Int. Conf. Human Factors in Manufacturing*, IFS 35–42.

Hutchin C. E. (2001). *Enterprise-focused management*. Thomas Telford, London.

Imai M. (1986). *Kaizen*. Random House, New York.

Ishikawa K. (1990). *Introduction to quality control*. Chapman and Hall.

Kakabadse A. and Parker C. (eds) (1984). *Power politics and organisations*. Wiley, Chichester.

Katz D. and Kahn R. L. (1978). *The social psychology of organisations*. 2nd ed., John Wiley, USA.

Katzenbach J. R. (1995). *Real change leaders*. Random House.

Kerlinger F. N. (1973). *Foundations of behavioural research*. 3rd ed., Holt Rinehart and Winston, New York.

Kolb D. A., Rubin I. M. and McIntyre J. M. (1971). *Organizational psychology an experiential approach*. 2nd ed., Prentice-Hall, New Jersey.

Kuhn T. S. (1970). *The structure of scientific revolutions*. 2nd ed., University of Chicago Press.

Lawrence P. R. and Lorsch J. W. (1967). *Organisation and environment*. Cambridge, MA, Harvard University Press.

Lee R. and Lawrence P. (1985). *Organisational behaviour – politics at work*. Hutchinson, London.

Leonard-Barton D. and Kraus W. A. (1985). Implementing New Technology. *Harvard Business Review*, Nov.–Dec., 102–109.

Levinson W. A. (1998). *Leading the way to competitive excellence*. ASQ, Wisconsin.

Lewin K. (1947). Frontiers in group dynamics: concept, method and reality in social science. *Human Relations* **1**(1), June, 5–41.

Likert R. (1967). *The human organisation*. McGraw Hill, New York.

McMullen T. B. (1998). *Theory of constraints management system*. St Lucie Press, Boca Raton.

Moore M. and Gergen P. (1985). Risk taking and organizational change. *Training and Development Journal*, **39**(6), 72–76.

Morgan G. (1986). *Images of organization*. Sage Publications, London.

Newell A. and Simon H. A. (1972). *Human problem solving*. Prentice-Hall, New Jersey.

Newman V. (1995). *Problem solving for results*. Gower, London.

Noreen E., Smith D. and Mackey J. T. (1995). *The Theory of Constraints and its implications for management accounting*. North River Press, Great Barrington, MA.

Pascale R. (1991). *Managing on the edge*. Penguin, London.

Paterson (1960) in Emery F. E. (1967). The case study method. *Tavistock Report*, Doc. No. 265, Tavistock Institute of Human Relations, London.

Pettigrew A. and Whipp, R. (1991). Managing change for competitive success. Blackwell Business, Oxford.

Pfeffer J. (1981). *Power in organizations*. Ballinger Publishing, Cambridge, Mass.

Pfeffer J. (1992). *Managing with power*. Harvard Business School Press, Boston, Mass.

Popper K. R. (1992). *The logic of scientific discovery*. Routledge, London.

Porter M. E. (1980). *Competitive strategy*. Free Press, New York.

Rapoport R. N. (1970). *Mid-career development*. Tavistock Publications, London.

Robson S. and Foster A. (1989). *Qualitative research in action*. Edward Arnold, London.

Ruelle D. (1991). *Chance and chaos*. Penguin, London.

Schein E. H. (1980). *Organizational psychology*. 3rd ed., Prentice Hall, London.

Scheinkopf L. J. (1999). *Thinking for a change*. St Lucie Press, Boca Raton.

Schonberger R. J. (1982). *Japanese manufacturing techniques*. Free Press, New York.

Schonberger R. J. (1986). *World class manufacturing*. Free Press, New York.

Selltiz C., Jahoda M., Deutsch M. and Cook S. W. (1966). *Research methods in social relations*. Methuen and Co. Ltd, London.

Skinner B. F. (1953). *Science and human behaviour*. The Free Press, London.

Skinner W. (1974). The focused factory. *Harvard Business Review*, May–June, 113–121.

Smith D. (2000). *The measurement nightmare*. St Lucie Press, Boca Raton.

Sommer B. and Sommer R. (1991). *A practical guide to behavioral research*. 3rd ed., Oxford University Press, London.

Stein R. E. (1996). *Re-engineering the manufacturing system*. Dekker, New York.

Strauss A. and Corbin J. (1990). *Basics of qualitative research*. Sage Publications, London.

Stuart R. (1983). Problems of training design. *Industrial and Commercial Training*, Aug. 239–240.

Tichy N. M. (1983). Managing organisational transformations. *Human Resource Management*, Spring/Summer, **22**, 1/2.

Umble M. M. and Srikanth M. L. (1990). *Synchronous manufacturing*. South-Western Publishing, Dallas.

VanGundy A. B. (1988). *Techniques of structured problem solving*. 2nd Ed., Van Nostrand Reinhold, New York.

Westwood R. (1995). Designing information systems for the management of operational priorities in batch manufacture. *Production Planning and Control*, **6**, 4, July–Aug., 286–300.

Wilensky, R. (1983). *Planning and understanding: a computational approach to human reasoning*. Addison-Wesley, Reading, Mass.

Womack J .P., Jones, D. T. and Roos D. (1990). *The machine that changed the world*. Rawson Associates, New York.

Wooldridge, E. (1982). *Negotiating technological change*. Personnel Management, Oct., 40–43.

Yin R. K. (1989). *Case study research design and methods*. Sage, London.

Index